ENERGY POLICIES, POLITICS AND PRICES

ENERGY TAXES

POLICY PERSPECTIVE AND ISSUES FOR CONSIDERATION

ENERGY POLICIES, POLITICS AND PRICES

Additional books in this series can be found on Nova's website under the Series tab.

Additional E-books in this series can be found on Nova's website under the E-book tab.

ENERGY POLICIES, POLITICS AND PRICES

ENERGY TAXES

POLICY PERSPECTIVE AND ISSUES FOR CONSIDERATION

NATHAN VIDET
EDITOR

NOVINKA
New York

For permission to use material from this book please contact us:
Telephone 631-231-7269; Fax 631-231-8175
Web Site: http://www.novapublishers.com

Additional color graphics may be available in the e-book version of this book.

Library of Congress Cataloging-in-Publication Data

ISBN: 978-1-62948-552-2

Published by Nova Science Publishers, Inc. † New York

CONTENTS

PREFACE

Since the 1970s, energy tax policy in the United States has attempted to achieve two broad objectives. First, policymakers have sought to reduce oil import dependence and enhance national security through a variety of domestic energy investment and production tax subsidies. Second, environmental concerns have led to subsidization of a variety of renewable and energy efficiency technologies via the tax code. While these two broad goals continue to guide policy, enacted policies that solely focus on achieving only one of the goals are often inconsistent with policies solely designed to achieve the other goal. For example, subsidies to oil and gas producers, while enhancing domestic oil and gas production, encourage an activity with negative environmental consequences. By providing a longitudinal perspective on energy tax policy and expenditures, this book examines how current revenue losses resulting from energy tax provisions compare to historical losses and provides a foundation for understanding how current energy tax policy evolved. Further, this book compares the relative value of tax incentives given to fossil fuels, renewables, and energy efficiency. Recent legislation has introduced, reintroduced, expanded, and extended a number of energy tax provisions. While a number of the current energy provisions have a long historical standing in the tax code, a wider variety of tax incentives, to promote a range of energy sources, are presently available than have been available in the past.

Chapter 1 - Examining trends in revenue losses associated with energy tax provisions provides insight into the actual direction of energy tax policy. In inflation-adjusted terms, revenue losses associated with energy tax provisions in the late 1970s and early 1980s are similar to revenue losses in the late 2000s. The composition of these revenue losses, however, has changed significantly. In the late 1970s nearly all revenue losses associated with energy tax provisions were the result of two tax preferences given to the oil and gas industry. In the early 1980s, revenue losses associated with special treatment for the oil and gas industry accounted for more than three quarters of all federal revenue losses associated with energy tax expenditures. Changes in policy, coupled with declining oil prices in the late 1980s, dramatically reduced revenue losses associated with oil and gas tax policy. Throughout the 1990s, the bulk of revenue losses associated with energy tax provisions were attributable to the tax credit for unconventional fuels. In the 2000s, revenue losses associated with renewable energy production incentives began to make up a larger portion of energy tax expenditure revenue losses. Revenue losses associated with tax provisions benefitting fossil fuels also remained important into the 2000s, with a large proportion of revenue losses in the mid-to-late 2000s associated with the unconventional fuel production credit, benefitting synthetic coal producers. In the late 2000s, the majority of revenue losses have been associated with incentives designed to promote alternative fuels and biofuels. By 2010, revenue losses associated with tax incentives for renewables exceeded revenue losses associated with fossil fuels. The Section 1603 grants in lieu of tax credits, made available starting in 2009, have resulted in increased federal financial support for renewables.

Chapter 2 - The scheduled expiration of a number of energy tax incentives means energy tax policy will likely be considered by the 113th Congress. Under current law, for example, renewable energy projects that begin construction after the end of 2013 will not qualify for the renewable energy production tax credit (PTC). A number of other energy tax incentives, including provisions to support building energy efficiency and renewable fuels, are also scheduled to expire at the end of 2013. In the past, expired and expiring energy tax provisions have been extended as part of "tax extender" legislation.

Energy tax policy may also be considered as part of comprehensive tax reform legislation in the 113th Congress. A base-broadening approach to tax reform might consider the elimination of various energy tax expenditures in conjunction with a reduction in overall tax rates. Alternative revenue sources, such as a carbon tax, may also be evaluated as part of the tax reform process.

The President's FY2014 budget proposes a number of changes to energy tax policy. The Obama Administration proposes to repeal a number of existing tax incentives for fossil fuels, while providing new or expanded incentives for alternative and advanced technology vehicles, renewable electricity, energy efficiency, and advanced energy manufacturing.

Energy tax policy involves the use of one of the government's main fiscal instruments, taxes (both as an incentive and as a disincentive) to alter the allocation or configuration of energy resources and their use. In theory, energy taxes and subsidies, like tax policy instruments in general, are intended either to correct a problem or distortion in the energy markets or to achieve some economic (efficiency, equity, or even macroeconomic) objective. The economic rationale for government intervention in energy markets is commonly based on the government's perceived ability to correct for market failures. Market failures, such as externalities, principal-agent problems, and informational asymmetries, result in an economically inefficient allocation of resources—in which society does not maximize well-being. To correct for these market failures governments can utilize several policy options, including taxes, subsidies, and regulation, in an effort to achieve policy goals. In practice, energy tax policy in the United States is made in a political setting, determined by fiscal dictates and the views and interests of the key players in this setting, including policymakers, special interest groups, and academic scholars. As a result, enacted tax policy embodies compromises between economic and political goals, which could either mitigate or compound existing distortions.

In: Energy Taxes
Editor: Nathan Videt
ISBN: 978-1-62948-552-2

Chapter 1

ENERGY TAX POLICY: HISTORICAL PERSPECTIVES ON AND CURRENT STATUS OF ENERGY TAX EXPENDITURES*

Molly F. Sherlock

SUMMARY

Since the 1970s, energy tax policy in the United States has attempted to achieve two broad objectives. First, policymakers have sought to reduce oil import dependence and enhance national security through a variety of domestic energy investment and production tax subsidies. Second, environmental concerns have led to subsidization of a variety of renewable and energy efficiency technologies via the tax code. While these two broad goals continue to guide policy, enacted policies that solely focus on achieving only one of the goals are often inconsistent with policies solely designed to achieve the other goal. For example, subsidies to oil and gas producers, while enhancing domestic oil and gas production, encourage an activity with negative environmental consequences.

* This is an edited, reformatted and augmented version of a Congressional Research Service publication, CRS Report for Congress R41227, dated May 2, 2011.

By providing a longitudinal perspective on energy tax policy and expenditures, this report examines how current revenue losses resulting from energy tax provisions compare to historical losses and provides a foundation for understanding how current energy tax policy evolved. Further, this report compares the relative value of tax incentives given to fossil fuels, renewables, and energy efficiency. Recent legislation has introduced, reintroduced, expanded, and extended a number of energy tax provisions. While a number of the current energy provisions have a long historical standing in the tax code, a wider variety of tax incentives, to promote a range of energy sources, are presently available than have been available in the past.

Examining trends in revenue losses associated with energy tax provisions provides insight into the actual direction of energy tax policy. In inflation-adjusted terms, revenue losses associated with energy tax provisions in the late 1970s and early 1980s are similar to revenue losses in the late 2000s. The composition of these revenue losses, however, has changed significantly. In the late 1970s nearly all revenue losses associated with energy tax provisions were the result of two tax preferences given to the oil and gas industry. In the early 1980s, revenue losses associated with special treatment for the oil and gas industry accounted for more than three quarters of all federal revenue losses associated with energy tax expenditures. Changes in policy, coupled with declining oil prices in the late 1980s, dramatically reduced revenue losses associated with oil and gas tax policy. Throughout the 1990s, the bulk of revenue losses associated with energy tax provisions were attributable to the tax credit for unconventional fuels. In the 2000s, revenue losses associated with renewable energy production incentives began to make up a larger portion of energy tax expenditure revenue losses. Revenue losses associated with tax provisions benefitting fossil fuels also remained important into the 2000s, with a large proportion of revenue losses in the mid-to-late 2000s associated with the unconventional fuel production credit, benefitting synthetic coal producers. In the late 2000s, the majority of revenue losses have been associated with incentives designed to promote alternative fuels and biofuels. By 2010, revenue losses associated with tax incentives for renewables exceeded revenue losses associated with fossil fuels. The Section 1603 grants in lieu of tax credits, made available starting in 2009, have resulted in increased federal financial support for renewables.

The federal government also loses revenue from excise tax credits given to alcohol fuel blenders (specifically, the volumetric ethanol excise tax credit (VEETC)). While excise tax credits are not technically a tax expenditure (technically, tax expenditures are only revenue losses associated with income tax provisions), these excise tax credits have played an important role in shaping energy tax policy and were estimated to result in revenue losses of $5.7 billion in 2010 alone.

Since the 1970s, energy tax policy in the United States has attempted to achieve two broad objectives. First, policymakers have sought to reduce oil import dependence and enhance national security through a variety of domestic energy investment and production tax subsidies. Second, environmental concerns have led to subsidization of a variety of renewable and energy efficiency technologies via the tax code. While these two broad goals continue to guide policy, enacted policies that solely focus on achieving only one of the goals are often inconsistent with policies solely designed to achieve the other goal. For example, subsidies to oil and gas producers, while enhancing domestic oil and gas production and ultimately increasing the burning of fossil fuels, encourage an activity which may have negative environmental consequences.

By providing a longitudinal perspective on energy tax policy and expenditures, this report examines how current revenue losses resulting from energy tax provisions compare to historical losses and provides a foundation for understanding how current energy tax policy evolved. Further, this report compares the relative value of tax incentives given to fossil fuels, renewables, and energy efficiency. Recent legislation has introduced, reintroduced, expanded, and extended a number of energy tax provisions. While a number of the current energy provisions have a long historical standing in the tax code, a wider variety of tax incentives, to promote a range of energy sources, are presently available than have been available in the past.

After reviewing the history of energy tax policy, this report examines the economic rationale for government interventions in energy markets. Understanding when and how government intervention can improve market outcomes assists in evaluating the potential effects of various tax policy proposals. In the case of energy markets, externalities, other market barriers, and national security concerns raise the possibility that government intervention via tax policy may lead to a more economically efficient distribution of energy resources.[1]

Trends in energy tax expenditures have changed substantially over the past 30 years.[2] In the early 1980s, revenue losses associated with energy tax provisions were approximately 3% of total revenue losses from all tax expenditures. In the mid-1980s, energy tax expenditures and total tax expenditures were scaled back. While total tax expenditures relative to GDP have trended up since the mid-1980s, energy tax expenditures relative to total tax expenditures have remained below early 1980s levels. Relatively low levels of tax expenditures do not necessarily suggest that the government is devoting fewer resources towards achieving energy policy goals, as federal grants, loans and loan guarantees, and mandates are also important energy policy tools.

Examining trends in revenue losses associated with energy tax provisions provides insight into the actual direction of energy tax policy. In inflation-adjusted terms, revenue losses associated with energy tax provisions in the late 1970s and early 1980s are similar in total cost to revenue losses in the late 2000s. The composition of these revenue losses, however, has changed significantly. In the late 1970s nearly all revenue losses associated with energy tax provisions were the result of two tax preferences given to the oil and gas industry. In the early 1980s, revenue losses associated with special treatment for the oil and gas industry accounted for more than three quarters of all federal revenue losses associated with energy tax expenditures. Changes in policy, coupled with declining oil prices in the late 1980s, dramatically reduced revenue losses associated with oil and gas tax policy. Throughout the 1990s, the bulk of revenue losses associated with energy tax provisions were attributable to the tax credit for unconventional fuels.[3] In the 2000s, revenue losses associated with renewable energy production incentives began to make up a larger portion of energy tax expenditure revenue losses, reaching an estimated 21% in 2006. Revenue losses associated with tax provisions benefitting fossil fuels also remained important into the 2000s, with a large proportion of revenue losses in the mid-to-late 2000s associated with the unconventional fuel production credit, benefitting synthetic coal producers. In the late 2000s, the majority of revenue losses have been associated with incentives designed to promote biofuels.

The federal government also loses significant revenue from excise tax credits given to alcohol fuel blenders (specifically, the volumetric ethanol excise tax credit (VEETC)). While excise tax credits are not technically a tax expenditure (technically, tax expenditures are only revenue losses associated with income tax provisions), these excise tax credits have played an important role in shaping energy tax policy. In 2010, tax credits for alcohol fuels reduced excise tax receipts by $5.7 billion.

In 2009, Congress enacted the Section 1603 grant in lieu of tax credit program as part of the American Recovery and Reinvestment Act (ARRA; P.L. 111-5).[4] The Section 1603 grant program allows taxpayers eligible for the renewable energy production tax credit (PTC) and investment tax credit (ITC) to elect to receive a one-time cash payment from the Treasury instead of tax payments. In 2010, outlays under this program were $4.2 billion.

A Brief History of Energy Tax Policy

The history of energy tax policy can be divided into five eras:[5] the oil and gas period from 1916 through 1970, the energy crisis period of the 1970s, the 1980s free-market era of the Reagan Administration, the post-Reagan era of the 1990s, and the 2000s, which is characterized by a renewed interest in promoting renewable energy.[6]

Energy Tax Policy from 1916 to 1970: Promoting Oil and Gas

For more than half a century, federal energy tax policy focused almost exclusively on increasing domestic oil and gas reserves and production. There were no tax incentives promoting renewable energy or energy efficiency. During that period, two major tax preferences were established for oil and gas. These two provisions speed up the capital cost recovery for investments in oil and gas exploration and production. First, the expensing of intangible drilling costs (IDCs) and dry hole costs was introduced in 1916.[7] This provision allows IDCs to be fully deducted in the first year rather than being capitalized and depreciated over time. Second, the excess of percentage over cost depletion deferral was introduced in 1926.[8] The percentage depletion provision allows a deduction of a fixed percentage of gross receipts rather than a deduction based on the actual value of the resources extracted.[9] Through the mid-1980s, these tax preferences given to oil and gas remained the largest energy tax provisions in terms of estimated revenue loss. Both of these provisions remain in the tax code in limited form today.

Energy Tax Policy in the 1970s: Energy Efficiency and Unconventional and Renewable Fuels

Events in the 1970s caused a dramatic shift in the focus of federal energy tax policy as evidenced by legislation enacted in the late 1970s and early 1980s.

PROVISIONS INTRODUCED UNDER THE ENERGY TAX ACT OF 1978 AND THE WINDFALL PROFIT TAX ACT OF 1980

Energy Tax Act of 1978 (ETA78)

- *Residential Energy Credits*: Homeowners were eligible to receive tax credits for installing energy efficiency property (such as insulation and weatherization components). Residential installations of solar, wind, and geothermal energy equipment were also eligible for tax credits.
- *Transportation*: A gas guzzler tax was imposed on a manufacturer's sale of automobiles that had a miles per gallon (mpg) rating below specified fuel economy standards.
- *Tax Subsidies for Alcohol Fuels*: Gasohol (a blend of gasoline and ethanol) became eligible to receive a partial excise tax exemption.
- *Business Energy Tax Credits*: Businesses were eligible to receive tax credits for investments in energy efficiency, renewable energy, or alcohol fuels property.
- *Percentage Depletion for Geothermal*: Expanded the option to expense intangible drilling and development costs for geothermal deposits.

Windfall Profit Tax Act of 1980 (WPT80)

- *Windfall Profit Tax*: The windfall profit tax was an excise tax on domestically produced crude oil.
- *Alternative (Unconventional) Fuel Production Credit*: Provided a credit to promote the domestic production of energy from unconventional fuel sources. Qualifying fuels included oil produced from shale or tar sands, gas produced from geopressurized brine, Devonian shale, tight formations, or coalbed methane, gas from biomass, and synthetic fuels from coal.
- *Tax-Exempt Interest on Industrial Development Bonds (IDBs)*: State and local electric utilities could issue tax-exempt bonds for the development of facilities producing fuel from solid waste.

First, large budget deficits made it difficult to continue the large tax preferences given to oil and gas. Second, the 1970s brought a heightened awareness of environmental issues, resulting in interest in promoting alternative energy sources alongside energy efficiency. Finally, the oil embargo and subsequent energy crisis of 1973, followed by the 1979 crisis in the wake of the Iranian Revolution, led policymakers to enact policies promoting alternative fuels (both alcohol and unconventional fuels) and energy efficiency. Additionally, policy also focused on increasing domestic energy production to enhance national energy security.

Three broad actions were taken through the tax code shifting energy policy away from oil and gas promotion towards creating incentives for alternative energy and efficiency. First, the oil industry's two major tax preferences—expensing of IDCs and percentage depletion—were significantly reduced. Second, several excise taxes penalizing the use of fossil fuels were introduced. These included the federal "gas guzzler" tax,[10] a windfall profit tax on oil,[11] and an excise tax on petroleum (the "Superfund" program).[12] Third, a number of tax incentives were implemented to promote energy efficiency and incentivize alcohol and unconventional fuels. Most of these new tax subsidies were introduced as part of the Energy Tax Act of 1978 (ETA78, P.L. 95-618). The Windfall Profit Tax Act of 1980 (WPT80; P.L. 96-223) also introduced a number of provisions that had the effect of either discouraging fossil fuel production or promoting unconventional (synthetic) or renewable fuels. In spite of these policy shifts, the majority of revenue losses associated with energy tax provisions served to benefit the oil and gas industry well into the 1980s. Since the 1970s, policymakers have continued to provide incentives for the development of both conventional and renewable forms of energy. In recent years, the policy focus has shifted more towards incentives for renewables. Policymakers have also continued to focus on providing incentives for energy efficient technologies in many different sectors. The residential energy efficiency tax credits, which were allowed to expire in the 1980s, were reenacted. A number of incentives for energy efficiency in commercial, industrial, and transportation sectors have been reinstated, expanded, or introduced.

Energy Tax Policy in the 1980s: The "Free-Market" Approach

The Reagan Administration sought to pursue what was believed to be a more neutral and less distortionary energy tax policy.[13] As such, the

Administration opposed using tax law to promote oil and gas development, energy efficiency, renewable energy sources, or unconventional or renewable fuels. It was believed that high oil prices alone would be enough to spur the economically efficient level of investment in unconventional or renewable energy sources.

Congress, in being consistent with the free market approach, allowed a number of the energy tax provisions enacted under the ETA78 to expire. Most business energy tax credits were allowed to expire in 1982 as scheduled. The residential energy tax credits were allowed to expire at the end of 1985 as scheduled. Of the ETA78 energy tax provisions scheduled to expire, only the tax credit for energy property (solar, geothermal, ocean geothermal, and biomass) was extended. Toward the end of President Reagan's second term, in 1988, following a massive decline in oil prices, the windfall profit tax (enacted under the WPT80) was repealed.

While the Reagan Administration did successfully reduce the number of energy tax provisions, the Administration did not accomplish all of their stated goals. Specifically, the primary tax incentives for oil and gas (expensing of IDCs and percentage depletion) were not eliminated, although they were scaled back as part of the Tax Reform Act of 1986 (TRA; P.L. 99-514).

In addition to a reduction in the number of favorable energy tax provisions, revenue losses associated with energy tax provisions fell during the 1980s due to relatively low energy prices. Low oil and gas prices during the late 1980s reduced investment. Consequently, revenue losses associated with tax provisions designed to promote investment in oil and gas declined.

Energy Tax Policy in the 1990s

In the post-Reagan era, energy tax policy again followed a more interventionist course. A number of provisions were enacted to promote energy production from renewable sources, alcohol fuels, and unconventional fuels. In addition, favorable tax provisions continued to be extended to the oil and gas industry.

The first major tax policies enacted under President George H. W. Bush were contained in the revenue provisions of the Omnibus Budget Reconciliation Act of 1990 (OBRA90; P.L. 101-508). First, the act increased the gasoline tax by 5¢ per gallon while also doubling the gas-guzzler tax. Second, the act introduced a 10% tax credit for enhanced oil recovery expenditures, liberalized some of the restrictions on the percentage depletion provision, and reduced the effect of the alternative minimum tax (AMT) on oil and gas investments. Third, the act expanded the unconventional fuel production credit and introduced a tax credit for small ethanol producers.

The Energy Policy Act of 1992 (P.L. 102-486) included a number of energy tax provisions. The tax credit for energy produced using renewable resources was established under this act. The renewable energy production tax credit (PTC) (IRC §45) was only available for electricity generated using wind or closed-loop biomass systems.[14] The act also included a number of other energy tax provisions, including an income tax deduction for the costs of clean-fuel powered vehicles, liberalization of the alcohol fuels tax credit, another expansion of the unconventional fuel production credit, and further liberalization of the favorable tax provisions for oil and gas. The Tax Relief and Extension Act, enacted as Title V of the Ticket to Work and Work Incentives Improvement Act of 1999 (P.L. 106-170), extended and liberalized the production tax credit, while also extending liberalizations regarding the percentage depletion provision for oil and gas.

In 1993, President Clinton proposed a differential British thermal unit (Btu) tax on fossil fuels,[15] which was ultimately dropped in favor of an excise tax increase on motor fuels. The Omnibus Budget Reconciliation Act of 1993 (OBRA93; P.L. 103-66) contained a 4.3¢ per gallon increase in the motor fuel excise tax. The revenues were allocated for deficit reduction rather than to the highway or other trust funds.

The late 1990s were characterized by low crude oil prices, which hurt oil producers and encouraged consumption. Additionally, with oil prices at record lows, there was little economic incentive to invest in energy efficiency, renewable energy, or renewable fuels.

Energy Tax Policy in the 2000s: A Renewed Interest in Renewables

Rising oil prices in the early 2000s led to a push for comprehensive energy legislation in the 107th and 108th Congresses. While comprehensive energy legislation was debated and otherwise stalled, energy tax policy goals were pursued through smaller provisions in tax relief and jobs bills. The Working Families Tax Relief Act of 2004 (P.L. 108-311) retroactively extended four energy tax subsidies that had been allowed to expire. These included (1) the tax credit for energy produced using renewable resources (PTC), (2) the suspension of the 100% net income limitation for the oil and gas percentage depletion allowance, (3) the tax credit for electric vehicles, and (4) the deduction for clean fuel vehicles. The American Jobs Creation Act of 2004 (P.L. 108-357) also included tax credits for alcohol fuels and biodiesel. Additionally, the act increased the number of technologies that were eligible for the renewable energy production tax credit.[16]

The Energy Policy Act of 2005 (EPACT05; P.L. 109-58) was the culmination of efforts for comprehensive energy legislation that began in 2001. (See the shaded text-box below for a listing and brief explanation of the energy tax provisions of EPACT05.) Spurred by rising energy prices and growing dependence on foreign oil, the law was shaped by competing concerns about energy security, environmental quality, and economic growth. Included in EPACT05 were a number of tax provisions related to energy infrastructure, domestic fossil fuels, energy efficiency, clean motor vehicles and fuels, among others.

EPACT05 was responsible for substantially increasing energy tax subsidies, both in terms of the number of provisions and amount of federal revenue losses. At the end of the 1990s, there were 11 energy tax expenditure programs listed in the President's Budget. The 2007 budget listed 38 energy tax expenditure programs.[17] The provisions enacted or modified under EPACT05 can be classified as those related to electricity infrastructure, domestic fossil fuels, energy efficiency, and clean motor vehicles and fuels.

The energy tax provisions contained within EPACT05 attempted to enhance domestic energy production and increase energy efficiency. The electricity infrastructure provisions included electricity generation incentives as well as those designed to facilitate the restructuring of the electric utility industry. Electricity market conditions (spiking prices, supply shortfalls, and transmission bottlenecks) led to the belief that incentives for investment in electricity generation and transmission were needed. Many of the domestic fossil fuel incentives were based on proposals that had been made in response to the low oil prices of the late 1990s. While oil prices had increased by 2005, EPACT05 still included a number of spending, tax, and deregulatory incentives to stimulate the production of oil and gas. The energy efficiency provisions of EPACT05 represented an effort to reduce energy consumption. EPACT05 reestablished some of the residential and business energy efficiency credits that had been allowed to expire in the 1980s as well as introduced a number of other energy efficiency incentives. Recognizing that transportation is the nation's largest energy consuming sector, EPACT05 expanded incentives for alcohol fuels and clean motor vehicles.

ENERGY TAX SUBSIDIES IN THE ENERGY POLICY ACT OF 2005 (EPACT05)[18]

Electricity Infrastructure

Extension and Modification of the Tax Credit for Renewable Electricity Production and Allow Pass-Through for Agricultural Cooperatives: The placed in service deadline was extended and the credit period was extended (to 10 years). Solar and refined coal were removed from the list of eligible property while hydropower and Indian coal were added. Allows eligible cooperatives to pass through the investment tax credit to patrons.

Clean Renewable Energy Bonds: Tax credit bonds were established to finance investment in clean renewable energy projects.

Treatment of Income of Certain Electrical Cooperatives: Extends provisions allowing electric cooperatives to treat certain income as member income.

Disposition of Transmission Property to Implement FERC Restructuring Policy: Special capital gains treatment of gains on the sale of certain electric transmission property extended.

Credit for Production from Advanced Nuclear Power Facilities: Credit is provided for energy produced at an advanced nuclear power facility.

Credit for Investment in Clean Coal Facilities: Investment credits established for investments in advanced coal and qualified coal gasification projects.

Electric Transmission Property Treated as 15-Year Property: Depreciable property used in the transmission of electricity for sale is classified as 15-year property under the Modified Accelerated Cost Recovery System (MACRS).

Expansion of Amortization for Certain Atmospheric Pollution Control Facilities: Certified air pollution control facilities used in connection with a coal-fired electric plant for plants in-service after January 1, 1976, qualify for 84-month amortization.

Modification to Special Rules for Nuclear Decommissioning Costs: Repeals the cost of service requirement for deductible contributions to a nuclear decommissioning fund and other limitations.

Five-Year NOL Carryback for Certain Electric Utility Companies: Certain electric companies are allowed to extend the Net Operating Loss (NOL) carryback period to five years.

Domestic Fossil Fuel Security

Extension of Credit for Producing Fuel from a Nonconventional Source for Facilities Producing Coke or Coke Gas: Production credit extended to facilities producing coke or coke gas.

Modification of Credit for Producing Fuel from a Nonconventional Source (Alternative Fuel Production Credit): The §29 credit is moved to become part of the general business credit, subjecting it to general business credit limitations.

Temporary Expensing for Equipment Used in Refining Liquid Fuels: Refineries are allowed to elect to expense 50% of the cost of qualified refinery property without limitation.

Pass Through Low Sulfur Diesel Expensing to Cooperative Owners: Allows cooperatives to pass through to stakeholders the immediate deduction (expensing) of capital costs incurred in complying with EPA sulfur regulations.

Natural Gas Pipelines Treated as 15-Year Property: Depreciable natural gas distribution lines given a 15-year recovery period under MACRS.

Natural Gas Gathering Lines Treated as Seven-Year Property: Natural gas gathering lines given a seven-year recovery period under MACRS.

Arbitrage Rules Not to Apply to Prepayments for Natural Gas: A safe harbor exception to the general rule that tax-exempt bond-financed prepayments violate arbitrage restrictions is established.

Determination of Small Refiner Exception to Oil Depletion Deduction: Increased the production limit such that larger producers, those with average daily refining of up to 75,000 barrels, can claim percentage depletion.

Amortization of Geological and Geophysical Expenditures: Geological and geophysical expenses paid or incurred in connection with domestic exploration for, or development of, oil and gas can be amortized over two years.

Energy Efficiency Provisions

Energy Efficient Commercial Buildings Deduction: A deduction is made available for taxpayer expenditures on energy- efficient property, including expenditures on energy-efficient lighting, heating, cooling, ventilation, hot water systems, or the building envelope, for commercial buildings.

Credit for Construction of New Energy Efficient Homes: Credit available to contractors for the construction of energy- efficient new homes.

Credit for Energy Efficient Improvements to Existing Homes (Credit for Nonbusiness Energy Property): Credit is made available to homeowners who install qualified energy-efficient property, including furnaces, boilers, windows, doors, insulation, or roofs, in existing homes.

Credit for Energy Efficient Appliances: Credit created for the production of energy-efficient dishwashers, clothes washers, and refrigerators.

Credit for Residential Energy Efficient Property: Individual tax credit for the purchase of solar electric, solar water heating, and qualified fuel cell property.

Credit for Business Installation of Qualified Fuel Cells and Stationary Microturbine Power Plants: Businesses eligible for tax credit for the installation of qualified fuel cell or qualified microturbine property.

Business Solar Investment Tax Credit: Increased credit rate to 30% for businesses investing in solar energy property.

Clean Motor Vehicle and Fuel Incentives

Alternative Motor Vehicle Credit: Provides an individual tax credit for new qualified fuel cell vehicles, new qualified advanced lean burn technology motor vehicles, new qualified hybrid motor vehicles, and new qualified alternative fuel motor vehicles.

Credit for the Installation of Alternative Fueling Stations: Businesses or individuals installing alternative fueling station property qualify for a tax credit.

Reduced Motor Fuel Excise Tax on Certain Mixtures of Diesel Fuel: Reduction of motor fuel excise tax for qualified mixtures of diesel-water fuel emulsion.

Extension of Excise Tax Provisions and Income Tax Credits for Biodiesel and Create Similar Incentives for Renewable Diesel: Extends existing income tax and excise tax credits as well as payment provisions for biodiesel. Extends tax credits available for biodiesel to renewable diesel (diesel derived from biomass).

Small Agri-Biodiesel Producer Credit and Modify Small Ethanol Producer Credit: Adds small agri-biodiesel producers to list of those eligible for biodiesel fuel credits. Raises the maximum production capacity for a small ethanol producer to 60 million gallons.

Additional Energy Tax Incentives

Expansion of Research Credit: Qualified energy research expenditures become eligible for the research credit.

Following EPACT05, additional incremental changes to energy tax policy were made in subsequent legislation. Provisions in the Tax Increase Prevention and Reconciliation Act (P.L. 109-222) reduced tax subsidies to oil and gas, while the Tax Relief and Health Care Act of 2006 (P.L. 109-432) extended a number of renewable energy provisions that were set to expire. The Food, Conservation, and Energy Act of 2008 (P.L. 110-234), otherwise referred to as the 2008 Farm Bill, contained a provision to promote cellulosic ethanol through a blenders credit.

The 2008 and 2009 stimulus bills expanded and extended energy tax incentives for renewables and efficiency. The Emergency Economic Stabilization Act of 2008 (EESA; P.L. 110-343) contained a number of energy tax provisions, primarily ones that extended existing provisions. The majority of the extended tax breaks went to promote renewable energy production, encourage energy efficiency, or provide incentives for alcohol fuels and clean motor vehicles. The cost of the energy tax extenders legislation in the Emergency Economic Stabilization Act of 2008 was fully financed, or paid for, by raising taxes on the oil and gas industry (mostly by reducing oil and gas tax breaks) and by other tax increases.

From the perspective of energy tax policy, the American Recovery and Reinvestment Act of 2009 (ARRA; P.L. 111-5) modified incentives for renewable energy production, energy efficiency, clean motor vehicles, as well as a number of other energy tax incentives.[19] Like EESA, most of ARRA focused on modifying and extending previously enacted energy tax provisions promoting renewables, efficiency, and alternative technology vehicles.

ARRA's Section 1603 grants for renewables, discussed in greater detail below, substantially changed federal incentives for renewable energy by converting the previously available tax credits into direct cash payments. ARRA also provided tax incentives for advanced energy manufacturing that were not previously available.

A number of energy tax provisions were scheduled to expire at the end of 2010, including the Section 1603 grants in lieu of tax credits program, the excise tax credits for alcohol fuels, and the tax credits for energy efficiency improvements to existing homes. Under the Tax Relief, Unemployment Reauthorization, and Job Creation Act of 2010 (P.L. 111-312), the Section 1603 grant program and the tax credits for alcohol fuels were extended for one year, through 2011. The tax credits for energy efficiency improvements to existing homes were also extended, but at a reduced rate.[20] The tax credits for advanced energy manufacturing were not extended in P.L. 111- 312.

ECONOMIC RATIONALE FOR INTERVENTION IN ENERGY MARKETS[21]

The primary economic justification for intervening in energy markets via the tax code is to address market failures. When market failures are present, resources are not efficiently allocated. Market failures can result from the presence of externalities, the existence of principal-agent problems or informational inefficiencies, or from a failure to adequately address national security concerns. The following paragraphs elaborate on these concepts in the context of energy taxation.

Both the production and consumption of energy often generate negative externalities.[22] For example, burning fossil fuels contributes to air pollution and generates greenhouse gasses. When an activity generates a negative externality, imposing a tax on the activity can improve economic efficiency. For example, driving gasoline powered motor vehicles may impose negative externalities due to polluting emissions as well as increased highway congestion. Imposing a tax equal in value to the monetary value of the driving-induced environmental and congestion damages reduces the equilibrium quantity of driving. By imposing a tax, potential drivers face a price of driving that is equal to the social marginal cost associated with driving. With a tax, an individual's choices regarding driving are based on their own costs as well as the external costs driving imposes on society.

As an alternative, policymakers often subsidize a substitute activity, one that is associated with fewer negative externalities. Following the example above, policymakers may choose to subsidize public transportation, reducing the price of public transportation relative to driving. Currently, there are a number of subsidies available for renewable energy production and technologies. While taxing activities associated with negative externalities may enhance economic efficiency, subsidizing the alternative activity is not necessarily economically efficient. Subsidizing renewable energy, in this context, reduces the average price of energy, which increases demand and ultimately consumption. Subsidies for renewable energy, by decreasing the average price of energy, work against initiatives for energy efficiency.[23] Further, the government must raise revenue to finance these subsidies. Such revenues may be raised using distortionary taxes.[24]

Intervention in energy markets has also been justified in the presence of principal-agent problems. Principal-agent problems occur when the ultimate consumer of energy does not make equipment purchasing decisions. For example, with rental property, landlords choose what appliances to install while tenants are often responsible for paying utility bills. Landlords may be unwilling to pay higher prices for energy-efficient appliances when the savings will ultimately accrue to tenants. Tax policies that reduce the cost of energy-efficient appliances tend to increase energy- efficient installations. Existing tax policies, however, do not directly aim to ameliorate the under- installation of energy-efficient property in markets that likely suffer from principal-agent problems (current energy tax incentives are not targeted toward markets susceptible to principal- agent problems, such as rental housing).

Informational problems and a variety of other market barriers may also be used to justify government intervention in energy markets. For example, homeowners may not know the precise payback or rate of return of a specific energy-efficient device. This may explain the so-called “energy paradox”—the empirical observation that consumers require an abnormally high rate of return to undertake energy-efficiency investments.[25] High initial first costs of energy-efficiency investments are also often cited as a barrier to investment in energy efficiency.[26] When externalities lead to an inefficient use of energy resources, tax policy may effectively address the inefficiency. It is less clear that tax policy will effectively address the inefficiency when informational problems or other barriers prevent an efficient allocation of energy resources. While tax subsidies can be used to reduce the cost of investing in energy-efficient property, informational programs or consumer lending programs may also be effective at encouraging investments in energy-efficiency.

Preserving national security is another often-cited rationale for intervention in energy markets. Presently, much of the petroleum consumed in the United States is derived from foreign sources.[27] There are potentially a number of external costs associated with petroleum importation, especially when imported from unstable countries and regions. First, a high level of reliance on imported oil may contribute to a weakened system of national defense or contribute to military vulnerability in the event of an oil embargo or other supply disruption. Second, there are costs to allocating more resources to national defense than otherwise necessary when relying on high levels of imported oil.[28] Specifically, there is an opportunity cost associated with resources allocated to national defense, as such resources are not available for other domestic policy initiatives and programs. To the extent that petroleum importers fail to take these external costs into account, there is market failure. While imposing a tax on imported oil would theoretically correct for this externality, in practice such a tax would likely violate trade agreements. Instead, policymakers have historically subsidized domestic oil and gas production.

The economic well-being and economic security of the nation depends on having stable energy sources. There are national economic costs associated with unstable energy supplies, such as increasing unemployment and inflation that may follow oil price spikes. While domestic production subsidies for oil and gas may reduce the cost of producing, such subsidies are unlikely to materially change consumer prices. Oil as a commodity is priced on world markets, and so long as the United States remains an open economy it will be affected by world oil price fluctuations. Even if the United States produces all the energy consumed domestically, world oil price fluctuations will impact the prices of other imported goods.

ENERGY TAX EXPENDITURES

The Congressional Budget and Impoundment Act of 1974 (the Budget Act; P.L. 93-344) defines tax expenditures as "revenue losses attributable to provisions of the federal tax laws which allow a special exclusion, exemption, or deduction from gross income or which provide a special credit, a preferential rate of tax, or a deferral of tax liability." Both the Treasury Department and the Joint Committee on Taxation (JCT) provide annual tax expenditure estimates. The Treasury's list is included in the President's annual budget submission.[29] The JCT issues annual tax expenditure estimates as a stand-alone product.

Tax provisions that reduce excise tax revenues are technically not considered tax expenditures under the Budget Act.[30] Tax provisions are only considered to have tax expenditure impacts if they lead to a reduction in corporate or personal income tax receipts. Consequently, excise tax credits are not considered tax expenditures. Even though excise tax credits or rate reductions are not technically considered tax expenditures, provisions that provide exemptions from, or credits against, excise taxes still reduce taxpayers' aggregate tax liability and lead to federal revenue losses. Grants paid by the Treasury are also not tax expenditures, as grants involve direct federal outlays rather than revenue losses attributable to reduced tax receipts.

Figure 1 illustrates the broader trend in tax expenditures from 1977 through 2010 as well as the trend in energy tax expenditures.[31] The solid line depicts revenue losses arising from tax expenditures as a percentage of GDP. Between 1977 and 1987 revenue losses associated with tax expenditures increased from less than 6% of GDP to nearly 10% of GDP. By reducing tax rates, eliminating and scaling back various tax expenditures, and generally broadening the tax base, the Tax Reform Act of 1986 (TRA86; P.L. 99-514) reduced revenue losses associated with tax expenditures. By 1989 revenue losses associated with tax expenditures were again less than 6% of GDP.

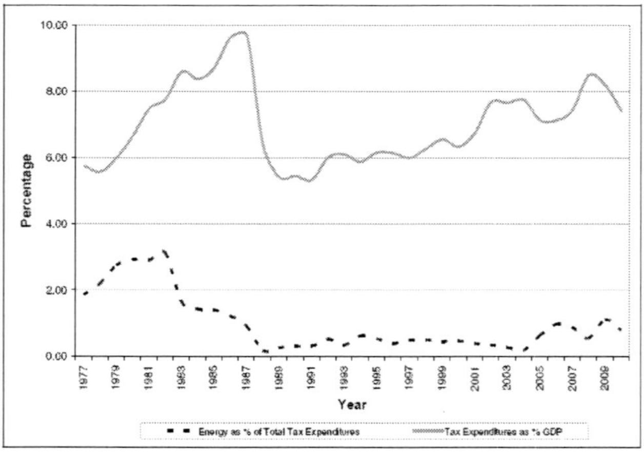

Source: CRS calculations using data from the Joint Committee on Taxation (JCT) and the Office of Management and Budget (OMB).

Figure 1. Energy and Tax Expenditures: 1977 – 2010.

Since the end of the 1980s, revenue losses associated with tax expenditures as a percentage of GDP have trended upward. The increase in revenue losses associated with tax expenditures partially reflects rising incomes during periods of economic expansion, but it is also the result of the introduction of new tax expenditures or the expansion of existing tax expenditure provisions.[32]

The dashed line in **Figure 1** depicts revenue losses associated with energy-related tax expenditures as a percentage of total tax expenditures. While tax expenditures as a percentage of GDP were high in relative terms in the late 1970s into the early 1980s, energy tax expenditures relative to total tax expenditures were also relatively high. In 1982, revenue losses from energy tax expenditures as a percentage of total tax expenditures exceeded 3%. By the end of the 1980s, revenue losses from energy tax expenditures as a percentage of total tax expenditures dropped to less than one-third of one percent (0.3%). Energy tax expenditures as a percentage of total tax expenditures have remained below 1% in all years except 2009 (energy tax expenditures as a percentage of total tax expenditures were estimated to be 1.1% in 2009). The reduced importance of energy tax expenditures may be reflective of a policy preference in which tax policy is not the preferred mechanism for achieving energy policy goals. In addition to tax incentives, there are a number of federal grants and energy-related mandates designed to achieve federal energy goals.[33] For example, ARRA's Section 1603 grant in lieu of tax credit program converted some of the federal support for renewable energy into a grant program not delivered directly through the tax code.

A Cautionary Note: The Non-Additive Nature of Tax Expenditures

Technically, tax expenditures cannot be simply summed to estimate the aggregate revenue loss because of interaction effects. When the revenue losses associated with various tax provisions are estimated, the estimates are made assuming that there are no changes in other provisions or in taxpayer behavior. Consequently, aggregate tax expenditure estimates, derived from summing the estimated revenue effects of individual tax expenditure provisions, are unlikely to reflect the actual change in federal receipts associated with removing various tax provisions.

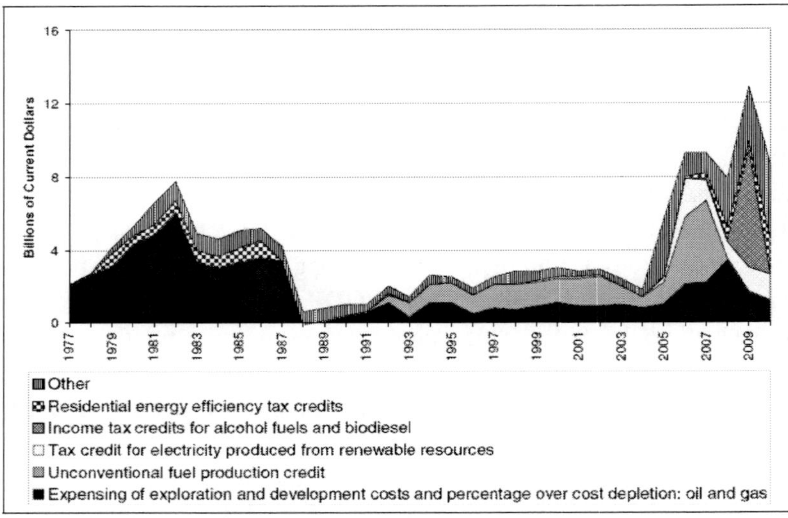

Source: CRS calculations using JCT tax expenditure estimates.

Notes: This figure does not include excise tax incentives or Section 1603 grants in lieu of tax credits.

Figure 2. Energy Tax Expenditures: Current Dollars (1977 – 2010).

(1977 – 2010)

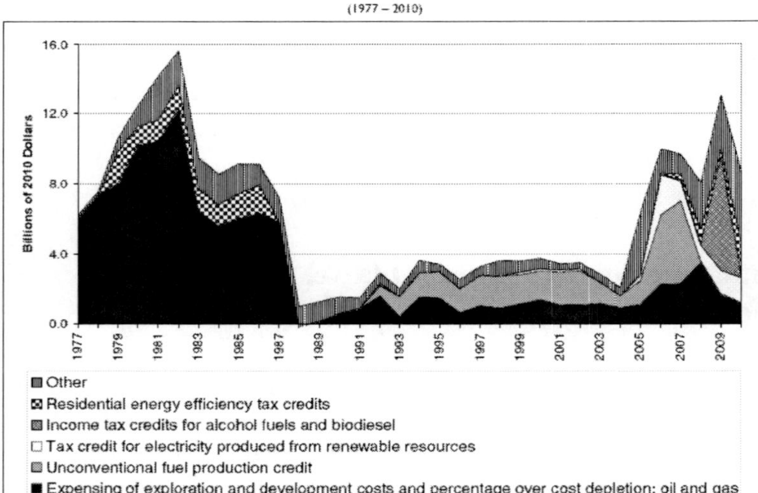

Source: CRS calculations using JCT tax expenditure estimates and data from the OMB.

Notes: Values were adjusted to 2010 dollars using the OMB's GDP price index. This figure does not include excise tax incentives or Section 1603 grants in lieu of tax credits.

Figure 3. Energy Tax Expenditures: Inflation-Adjusted Dollars.

While a summation of tax expenditure revenue loss estimates may not be technically accurate, the analysis presented here likely provides a useful approximation of the general trend in energy tax expenditures. It is unknown whether the summing of individual tax expenditure provisions understates or overstates actual revenue losses associated with tax expenditures.[34] Furthermore, since many tax expenditure provisions remain in the tax code minimally changed for long periods of time, the bias from summing tax expenditures remains approximately the same from year to year. Even if the summation of tax expenditures is not believed to represent accurate levels of revenue loss, the examination of trends is still highly useful.

A Closer Look at Energy Tax Expenditures

Figure 2 illustrates trends in energy tax expenditures in current dollars from 1977 through 2010. **Figure 3** presents energy tax expenditures using inflation-adjusted dollars. Through the 1970s and most of the 1980s the majority of tax expenditures benefited the oil and gas industry through the expensing of IDCs and percentage depletion provisions. In 1977, before the enactment of the ETA78, annual revenue losses of the expensing of IDCs and percentage depletion provisions to the oil and gas industry were more than $2 billion ($6 billion in 2010 dollars).

While the ETA78 and WPT80 enacted energy tax provisions to encourage efficiency and unconventional and renewable fuels, the majority of energy tax expenditures continued to result from the expensing of IDCs and percentage depletion provisions for oil and gas. In 1981, these two oil and gas tax provisions resulted in revenue losses of $4.9 billion while the residential energy efficiency credits resulted in revenue losses of $0.5 billion ($10.5 billion and $1.2 billion in 2010 dollars, respectively). The majority of the $1.2 billion for "other" energy tax expenditures were attributable to the expensing of IDCs and percentage depletion provisions for fuels other than gas and the energy credit for investment in renewable energy production.

Expensing of IDCs and Percentage Depletion for Oil and Gas

While a number of energy tax incentives were allowed to expire under the Reagan Administration, the most striking change in energy tax expenditures came toward the end of the 1980s. By 1988, energy tax expenditures were only $0.6 billion ($1 billion in 2010 dollars). Part of the reason for this relatively low estimate for revenue losses is the negative tax expenditure estimate ($-0.6 billion) associated with the expensing of IDCs for oil and gas. While the tax incentives for oil and gas were scaled back under the TRA in 1986, external market forces, specifically low oil prices, were also responsible for the reduction in energy tax expenditures during the late 1980s that persisted into the 1990s.

The tax expenditure estimate for the expensing of IDCs provision can be negative—indicating an increase in federal revenues rather than a loss—since the provision represents a tax deferral, essentially an interest free loan from the government. Government revenue losses from the expensing of IDCs are incurred when an investment is made, as the costs are expensed in the first year. Over the next four years, however, there is an offsetting gain for the government, as no further deductions on investments can be made. When investments are growing, the additional amount deducted via expensing exceeds the offsetting gains from reduced cost depletions, and the government faces revenue losses. Investments in oil and gas fell off following the collapse of oil prices in 1986. In 1988 and 1989, the tax expenditure estimates for the expensing of IDCs provision were negative, indicating an increase in federal revenues. Throughout the 1990s and into the 2000s, the estimated revenue losses associated with this provision remained relatively small.

Unconventional Fuels Tax Credit

Throughout the 1990s, growth in energy tax expenditures was primarily driven by the unconventional fuel production credit (IRC § 29). In 1990, the two major oil and gas provisions, expensing of IDCs and percentage depletion, accounted for $0.4 billion in tax expenditures ($0.6 billion in 2010 dollars) while the remaining $0.6 billion ($0.9 billion in 2010 dollars) in revenue losses was attributable to a variety of other provisions, some for renewable energy and others for fossil fuel energy sources. By 1999, estimated revenue losses from expensing of IDCs and percentage depletion for oil and gas was $0.9 billion while the estimated revenue losses from the unconventional fuel production credit were $1.3 billion ($1.1 and $1.7 billion in 2010 dollars, respectively). Between 1990 and 1999, total energy tax expenditures had increased from $1 billion to $2.8 billion ($1.5 to $3.6 billion in 2010 dollars).

While the unconventional fuel production tax credit was initially enacted as part of the WPT80, the early revenue losses associated with the provision were low. The goal of the unconventional fuel production tax credit was to stimulate the production of synthetic fuels using domestic deposits of oil, gas, and coal. Even in the face of the high oil prices of the late 1970s and early 1980s, there was little production of unconventional fuels. By the late 1980s and into the early 1990s, producers of unconventional gases, such as coal bed methane and tight sands gas, had begun to claim the credit. The credit was expanded and extended under OBRA in 1990 and again under the Energy Policy Act of 1992.

The composition of energy tax expenditures remained relatively stable throughout the late 1990s and early 2000s. By 2005, significant changes in the composition of revenue losses attributable to energy tax expenditures began to emerge. As provisions enacted under EPACT05 in 2005 went into effect, revenue losses associated with energy tax provisions increased. The provision primarily responsible for increasing energy tax expenditures in the years immediately after 2005 was the unconventional fuel production credit. In 2004, revenue losses associated with the unconventional fuel production credit were an estimated $0.6 billion. By 2007, revenue losses associated with the provision had increased more than seven-fold to $4.5 billion.

The unconventional fuels production credit was designed to induce the substitution of coal for oil and stimulate the development of a new synthetic fuel industry, but ultimately there were questions as to whether the credit served to benefit its intended recipients. A number of favorable private letter rulings from the IRS in the late 1990s and early 2000s encouraged an increasing number of producers to claim the tax credit for synthetic fuels.[35] To qualify for the credit for coal- based synthetic fuel, producers had to demonstrate that their process involved a "substantial chemical change." Some firms qualifying for this credit were simply spraying newly mined coal with diesel fuel, pine-tar resin, limestone, acid, or some other substance to induce this chemical change. By the mid-2000s there was evidence of substantial abuse of the credit.[36] Following EPACT05, the Section 29 credit was eliminated from the Internal Revenue Code. Non-expired incentives for unconventional fuels are now claimed as part of the general business credit, under § 45K, and subject to overall limitations.

Renewable Energy Production Tax Credit

Revenue losses associated with the tax credit for electricity produced from renewable resources also grew relatively rapidly following 2005. While first introduced under the Energy Policy Act of 1992, revenue losses associated with the provision were negligible until 2005. In 2004, the American Jobs Creation Act expanded the list of technologies eligible for the credit. The eligibility of additional technologies, rising oil prices spurring investment in renewables, and a greater interest in reducing the use of fossil fuels, were all factors likely contributing to additional claims of the renewable energy production credit. By 2006, 23% ($2.1 billion) of estimated energy tax expenditures were attributable to the renewable energy production tax credit.

The primary tax incentives for renewable energy were substantially altered with the introduction of the Section 1603 grants in lieu of tax credits under ARRA.[37] Effectively, this provision allows PTC-eligible projects to instead receive a one-time payment from the Treasury in lieu of tax benefits. As of March 31, 2011, $6.9 billion had been paid out in Section 1603 grants.[38] Under current law, Section 1603 grants will not be available to projects with a construction start date after December 31, 2011.

Energy Efficiency Incentives

A number of residential and commercial energy efficiency tax incentives that had been allowed to expire in the 1980s were reintroduced under EPACT05. Over time, the share of energy tax expenditures supporting residential energy efficiency has fluctuated. In the early 1980s, tax expenditures associated with residential energy efficiency exceeded $0.5 billion, and represented about 9% of all energy-related tax expenditures. In 2007 the revenue losses for residential energy efficiency, the largest of the efficiency tax provisions enacted under EPACT05, were estimated to be $0.3 billion, or 3% of all energy tax expenditures. By 2010, estimated revenue losses for residential energy tax provisions had increased to $1.9 billion, or 22% of all energy tax expenditures.

The recent increase in the share of energy tax expenditures supporting residential energy efficiency can be attributed to the increased generosity of these tax credits under ARRA. Specifically, during 2009 and 2010, certain residential energy efficiency improvements were eligible for a 30% tax credit, up to $1,500. While the tax credits for residential energy efficiency improvements were extended through 2011 under the Tax Relief, Unemployment Reauthorization, and Job Creation Act of 2010 (P.L. 111-312), the credit rate was reduced to 10% and the credit capped at $500.

Tax Expenditures for Renewable Fuels

The most striking change in the composition of energy tax expenditures in the 2000s is the dramatic increase in the estimated revenue losses associated with the tax credits for alcohol fuels and biodiesel. This increase is primarily attributable to "black liquor." In the context of taxes, the term "black liquor" currently refers to a process in which pulp mills use a mixture of conventional fuel (such as diesel fuel) and a byproduct of the pulping process as an energy source for the mill. Prior to 2010, black liquor qualified for an income tax credit under the alternative fuel mixture tax credit.[39] The intent of this credit was not to provide a tax subsidy for black liquor, but instead to create incentives for companies producing liquid motor fuels from biomass. When enacted, this provision was estimated to cost less than $100 million annually. In the first half of 2009, $2.5 billion in tax credits were claimed.[40]

In 2009, an estimated 50% of energy tax expenditures were revenue losses associated with tax credits for alcohol fuels, with the vast majority of these credits going to producers using black liquor. The alcohol fuel mixture credit was allowed to expire at the end of 2009. The IRS subsequently ruled that black liquor qualifies for the cellulosic biofuel producer credit, which does not expire until the end of 2012. Under the Reconciliation Act of 2010 (P.L. 111-152), Congress modified the cellulosic biofuel producer credit such that fuels with significant water, sediment, or ash content, such as black liquor, were no longer eligible.[41] This healthcare reform pay-for reduced estimated tax expenditures associated with this provision by $23.6 billion over the 2010 through 2019 budget window.[42]

COMPARING TAX EXPENDITURES FOR FOSSIL FUELS, RENEWABLES, AND EFFICIENCY

Figure 4 provides a comparison of the relative magnitude of revenue losses associated with tax incentives for fossil fuels, renewables, and energy efficiency over time (**Appendix A** provides information on how various energy tax provisions are categorized).[43] The data in **Figure 4** are presented in inflation-adjusted dollars.

In the late 1970s, all revenue losses associated with energy tax expenditures provided benefits to fossil fuels, primarily oil, gas, and coal. Following the enactment of ETA78 and WPT80, revenue losses associated with tax provisions providing incentives for renewables and efficiency increased, but remained small relative to revenue losses associated with tax preferences for fossil fuels (in 1982, revenue losses associated with tax expenditures for renewables and efficiency were approximately 18% of those associated with tax preferences for fossil fuels). From the late 1980s through the early 2000s, not only were revenue losses associated with energy tax provisions low relative to previous and current levels, revenue losses associated with renewables and efficiency also made up a small proportion of total energy tax expenditures.

(1977 – 2010)

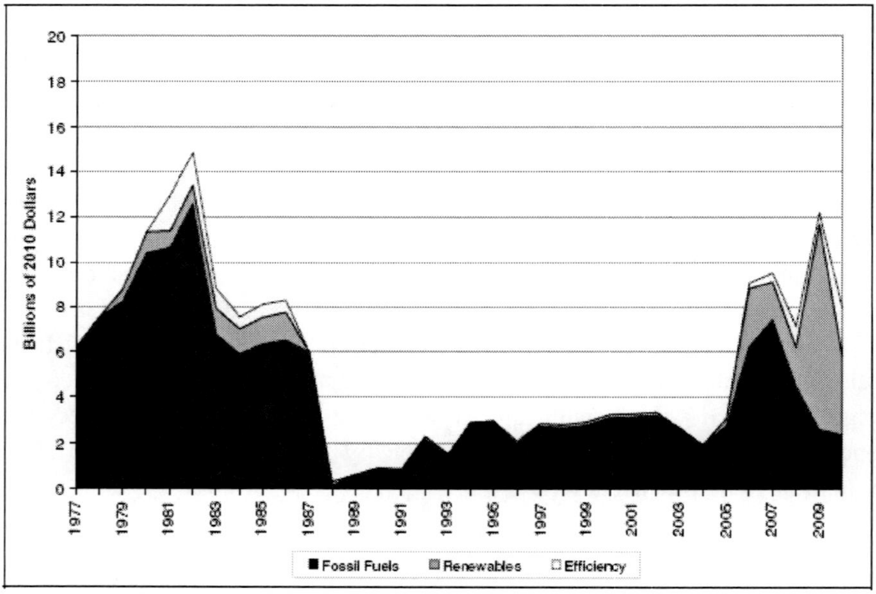

Source: CRS calculations using JCT tax expenditure estimates and data from the OMB.

Notes: Tax expenditures beyond 2009 are estimates and do not reflect legislation enacted after September 30, 2009. Values are adjusted to 2009 dollars using the OMB's GDP price index. This figure does not include excise tax incentives or Section 1603 grants in lieu of tax credits.

Figure 4. Tax Expenditures: Incentives for Fossil Fuels, Renewables, and Efficiency.

In the mid-2000s, revenue losses associated with energy tax provisions for renewables increased rapidly. Revenue losses associated with fossil fuels also increased in the mid-2000s. This increase was driven by the unconventional fuel production credit. By 2006, revenue losses associated with renewables were an estimated $2.6 billion (in 2010 dollars) while revenue losses associated with incentives for fossil fuels were an estimated $6.2 billion (in 2010 dollars). In 2006, the majority of the revenue losses associated with incentives for renewables were attributable to the renewable energy PTC.

The large increase in the estimated revenue losses associated with tax incentives for renewables in 2009 is attributable to "black liquor" under the alcohol fuel mixture tax credit. As noted above, producers whose production processes rely on black liquor are no longer eligible for the alternative fuel mixture tax credit or the cellulosic biofuel producer credit.

By 2010, the balance of energy tax expenditures had shifted such that tax expenditures supporting renewables were estimated to exceed those supporting fossil fuels. Estimates suggest that in 2010, 39% ($3.4 billion) of energy tax expenditures supported renewables. An estimated 28% ($8.7 billion) supported fossil fuels. As is discussed in greater detail below, when excise tax credits for alcohol fuels, biodiesel, and the Section 1603 grants in lieu of tax credits are included, an even larger share of federal tax support for energy can be attributed to renewables.

Taken together, **Figure 2**, **Figure 3**, and **Figure 4** emphasize the trends in energy tax policy over the last 30 years. The value of tax subsidies given to oil and gas through the expensing of IDCs and percentage depletion were dramatically reduced in the late 1980s. Following a period of relatively low levels of energy tax expenditures, revenue losses associated with energy tax provisions have increased, reaching levels similar to those experienced during and immediately following the "energy crisis" of the late 1970s. While the goal of energy tax policy has been to promote renewables and efficiency, the majority of revenue losses associated with energy tax expenditures in recent years have been associated with credits for unconventional or alcohol fuels. Even more striking is the fact that the primary beneficiaries of these tax credits—in both the case of the unconventional fuels production credit and the case of black liquor—were not those policymakers drafting the provision initially sought to subsidize.

OTHER ENERGY TAX PROVISIONS

As noted above, excise tax credits and various other tax-related revenue losses are not considered tax expenditures. Consequently, the excise tax credit for alcohol fuel mixtures—also known as the "blenders credit"—does not appear in conventional estimates of energy tax expenditures. The biodiesel producer tax credit, which results in a reduction in excise tax receipts, is also not included in the tax expenditure estimates above. Finally, Treasury grants in lieu of the renewable energy investment tax credit (ITC) or production tax credit (PTC), enacted under Section 1603 of the Recovery Act (ARRA), are not directly included in the tax expenditure estimates above. **Figure 5** illustrates the magnitude of revenue losses due to tax expenditures as defined above relative to revenue losses from reduced excise tax receipts and outlays associated with the Treasury grants in lieu of tax credits in inflation-adjusted dollars.

(1980 – 2010)

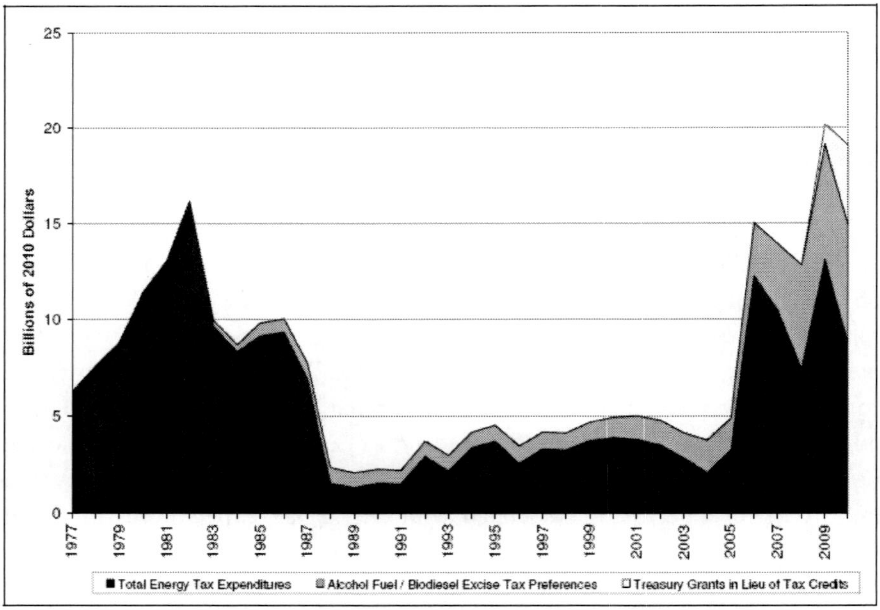

Source: CRS calculations using JCT and OMB tax expenditure estimates.

Notes: Values are adjusted to 2010 dollars using the OMB's GDP price index. Revenue losses associated with excise tax credits for alcohol fuels include are primarily due to tax credits for ethanol blenders. Revenue loss estimates for alcohol fuels excise tax credits also include revenue losses associated with credits for biodiesel in 2008, 2009, and 2010. Revenue loss estimates for excise tax credits are presented as reported by the OMB in the President's Budget. Excise tax revenue losses only reflect the reduction in excise tax receipts, and not any federal income tax offsets.

Figure 5. Energy Tax Expenditures and Fuel Credits: Inflation-Adjusted Dollars.

Alcohol Fuels

Over the past 30 years, tax incentives for alcohol fuels have resulted in substantial federal revenue losses. Most of the revenue losses associated with alcohol fuels have been realized either through excise tax exemptions or credits. Such exemptions or credits, however, do not show up as a tax expenditure, as these provisions do not directly reduce income tax liability.

Tax incentives for alcohol fuel blends were first enacted under ETA78. Under ETA78, alcohol fuels blends received a partial exemption from the excise tax on gasoline. The American Jobs Creation Act of 2004 (P.L. 108-357) restructured the tax subsidies for alcohol fuels. First, the blenders income tax credit was eliminated (since this credit was not as valuable as the excise tax exemption, the primary benefits for alcohol fuels were realized through the excise tax exemption, not the income tax credit). Second, the blenders excise tax exemption was replaced with the volumetric ethanol excise tax credit (VEETC).[44] From the perspective of alcohol fuel blenders, the change from an exemption to a credit increased the value of this tax provision.[45]

Excise tax revenue losses increased following the change from an excise tax exemption to an excise tax credit.[46] In 2004, an estimated $1.45 billion ($1.67 billion in 2010 dollars) in revenue was lost due to the excise tax exemption. In 2006, an estimated $2.57 billion ($2.77 billion in 2010 dollars) in revenue was lost due to the excise tax credit. By 2010, estimated revenue losses associated with the excise tax credit were $5.68 billion. The VEETC is set to expire at the end of 2011.

Biofuels

The American Jobs Creation Act of 2004 (P.L. 108-357) also created an excise tax credit for biodiesel. In 2009, estimated revenue losses associated with the biodiesel excise tax credit were $0.81 billion. The biodiesel mixture credit terminated on December 31, 2009, but was retroactively extended through the end of 2011 in the Tax Relief, Unemployment Reauthorization, and Job Creation Act of 2010 (P.L. 111-312).

To provide an additional comparison of revenue losses associated with tax preferences for fossil fuels, renewables, and efficiency, revenue losses associated with the excise tax credits for alcohol fuels and biodiesel are incorporated into **Figure 4**, presented earlier in this report. Including excise tax exemptions for alcohol fuels and biodiesel increases revenue losses for renewables relative to revenue losses for fossil fuels and efficiency, with the most dramatic shift taking place in the mid-2000s (see **Figure 6**). When revenue losses associated with excise tax preferences are included, estimated revenue losses associated with tax provisions benefiting renewables exceed estimated revenue losses associated with provisions benefiting fossil fuels in 1988-1989 and again in 2008. In 2008, estimated revenue losses associated with provisions benefitting renewables (including alcohol fuels) were an estimated 1.6 times estimated revenue losses benefitting fossil fuels.[47]

(1977 – 2010)

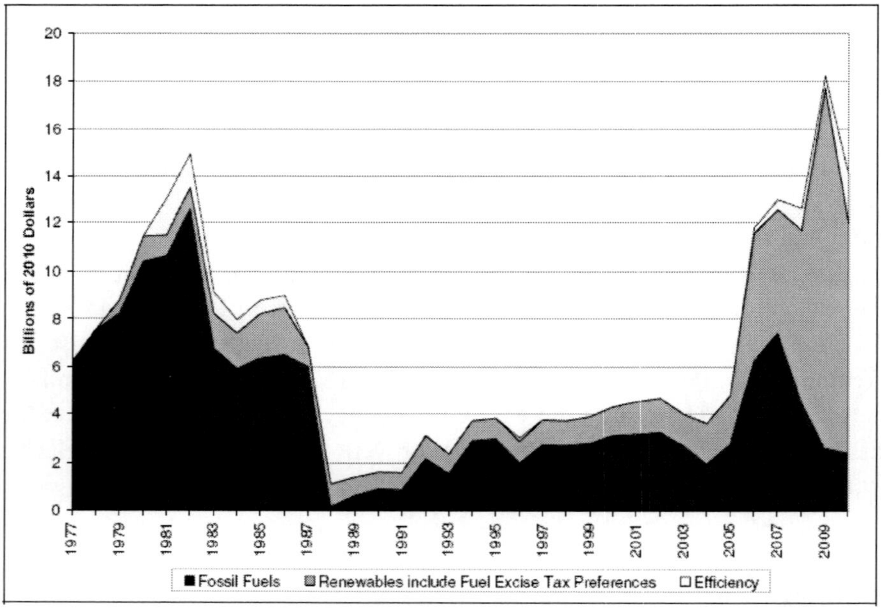

Source: CRS calculations using JCT and OMB tax expenditure estimates.

Notes: Values are adjusted to 2010 dollars using the OMB's GDP price index. Revenue loss estimates for excise tax credits are presented as reported by the OMB in the President's Budget. Excise tax revenue losses only reflect the estimated reduction in excise tax receipts, and not any federal income tax offsets.

Figure 6. Revenue Losses from Tax Expenditures and Excise Tax Provisions: Fossil Fuels, Renewables, and Efficiency.

Grants in Lieu of Tax Credits[48]

Under Section 1603 of ARRA, qualifying commercial renewable energy projects have the option of electing to receive a one-time cash grant from the Treasury in lieu of the renewable energy PTC or ITC. In the wake of the financial crisis, many renewable power project developers and their investors were less able to take advantage of existing tax credits for renewable energy projects. The grant in lieu of tax credit program was designed to provide an incentive for renewable energy development during the economic slowdown, where there was diminished demand for tax incentives. Currently, for projects to be eligible for the grant in lieu of tax credits, construction has to begin before the end of 2011.

The President's FY2012 Budget reports that $4.21 billion was awarded in grants under Section 1603 in 2010.[49] Between 2010 and 2016, it is estimated that the total effect on outlays of the Section 1603 Treasury grant program will be $18.95 billion.

(1977 – 2010)

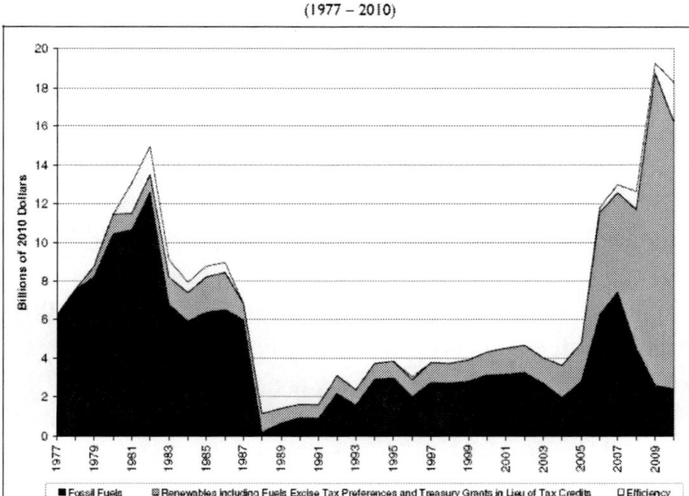

Source: CRS calculations using JCT and OMB tax expenditure estimates.

Notes: Values are adjusted to 2010 dollars using the OMB's GDP price index. Revenue loss estimates for excise tax credits are presented as reported by the OMB in the President's Budget. Excise tax revenue losses only reflect the estimated reduction in excise tax receipts, and not any federal income tax offsets.

Figure 7. Revenue Losses from Tax Expenditures, Excise Tax Provisions, and Treasury Grants in Lieu of Tax Credits: Fossil Fuels, Renewables, and Efficiency.

Figure 7 presents data on tax expenditures, including fuel excise tax provisions and outlays resulting from the Section 1603 grant program. When the excise tax provisions for alcohol fuels, biodiesel, and Section 1603 grant outlays are included, the cost associated with tax provisions for renewables is an estimated $13.78 billion for 2010. The value of fossil fuel tax expenditures in 2010 is an estimated $2.4 billion. Including these tax provisions, the cost of tax provisions that support renewables is roughly six times greater than the cost of provisions that support fossil fuels.

CONCLUSION

Since the 1970s, energy tax policy has attempted to achieve two broad objectives. First, policymakers have sought to reduce oil import dependence by subsidizing domestic sources of energy. Second, environmental concerns have motivated tax preferences for various renewable energy sources and energy efficiency. Using estimated federal revenue losses associated with energy tax provisions, it is not clear that energy tax policy in practice has followed a stable course consistent with these objectives.

The low levels of energy tax subsidization in the late 1980s and throughout the 1990s, coupled with periods of relatively low oil prices, did little to promote the development of domestic energy resources, renewable or otherwise. The overall level of tax subsidization of domestic energy resources in the mid-to-late 2000s was similar to early 1980s levels (in inflation-adjusted terms).

During the late 1980s, throughout the 1990s, and into the 2000s, revenue losses associated with energy tax provisions were low, both relative to total tax expenditures and relative to current energy tax expenditure levels. Since 2005, revenue losses associated with the renewable energy production tax credit have been increasing, suggesting an increase in renewable energy production and domestic renewable energy capacity. By 2010, revenue losses associated with tax incentives for renewables exceeded those available for fossil energy resources.

While environmental concerns have led to an increasing number of tax incentives for renewables and efficiency being made available, energy tax expenditures still suggest that, even in recent years, fossil fuels remain subsidized in practice.

Since the late 1970s, tax subsidies for oil and gas have been scaled back and made less generous, but revenue losses attributable to fossil fuel subsidies persisted through 2007. Overall, the number of energy tax provisions has increased since the 1970s, providing tax incentives to a broader spectrum of energy-related activities. In 2007, even with an increasing number of tax provisions designed to promote renewables and efficiency in place, the majority of energy tax expenditure revenue losses still served to benefit fossil fuels. In 2007, nearly half of the energy tax expenditure revenue losses were attributable to the unconventional fuel production credit being claimed by coal-based synfuel producers.

Following the expiration of the unconventional fuel credit in 2007, energy tax policy, as evaluated according to revenue losses, appears to have shifted towards favoring renewables. While revenue losses associated with the excise tax credit for alcohol fuels (ethanol) and the renewable energy production tax credit have increased in relative importance, most of the revenue losses categorized as being associated with renewables are attributable to "black liquor."

The fact that the tax provisions associated with the largest estimated revenue losses in the 2000s—the unconventional fuel tax credit claimed by synfuel producers and the alcohol fuels and cellulosic biofuels income tax credit claimed by those using "black liquor"—had high revenue loss stemming from claims that were inconsistent with policymakers' intent, raises concerns about using the tax code to achieve energy policy objectives. Designing tax policy that is more consistent with economic objectives could help address these concerns.

Energy tax policy, particularly in the 2000s, has focused on subsidizing a variety of clean-energy alternatives, an approach that is unlikely to maximize economic efficiency. Taxing energy-related activities that generate negative externalities (such as the burning of fossil fuels), as opposed to subsidizing clean-energy alternatives, would likely enhance the efficiency of energy tax policy.

Taxing an activity that imposes negative externalities reduces the amount of the activity in equilibrium, as a corrective tax leads market participants to consider the full internal and external costs of the activity when making consumption or production choices. Taxing activities that generate negative externalities also allows the government to avoid "picking winners," which is often the result when selective subsidies are given to certain sectors within the complete set of alternatives.

To provide subsidies, the government must generate revenue. If that revenue is generated by levying distortionary taxes in other sectors of the economy, such as income taxes that lead individuals to reduce work hours, such a policy is unlikely to be economically efficient. The government may be creating inefficiencies in the labor market via income taxes to finance subsidies for clean-energy alternatives. Taxing energy-related activities that generate negative externalities, increasing the price of activities associated with negative externalities relative to the clean-energy alternatives, would also create incentives for increased investment in and utilization of the clean-energy alternative without creating distortions in other markets.

Finally, limiting selective subsidies would reduce the scope for taxpayers to find loopholes allowing them to exploit energy tax incentives. Both coal-based synfuel producers and "black liquor" claimants were able to make small modifications in what were currently utilized production techniques, modifications which resulted in billions of dollars of tax incentives. Clean-energy tax subsidies do create incentives for alternative and innovative energy resources.

Congress, in drafting tax policy, however, faces significant challenges. Creating narrowly defined clean-energy tax policy may stifle innovation, while providing broader incentives leaves open the possibility of tax loopholes and potential abuse.

APPENDIX A. DATA TABLES

Table A-1 provides data from a sample of cross sections used to create **Figure 2**. Additional data regarding revenue losses associated with a specific tax provisions are available from the author upon request.

Table A-2 presents the estimated revenue losses associated with various tax provisions presented in **Table A-1**, adjusted for inflation. This information was used in creating **Figure 3** and **Figure 5**. Again, additional data regarding revenue losses associated with a specific tax provisions are available from the author upon request.

Table A-3 presents estimated revenue losses associated with various energy tax provisions. The provisions are categorized as those that benefit fossil fuels,[50] those that benefit renewables (both electricity and fuels),[51] and those that promote efficiency.[52] Fuels excise tax preferences include excise tax provisions for alcohol fuels, biodiesel, and renewable diesel.

Table A-1. Energy Tax Expenditures, Excise Tax Credits, and Grants in Lieu of Tax Credits: Current Dollars (billions of dollars)

	1977	1981	1985	1989	1993	1997	2001	2005	2007	2009	2010
Energy Tax Expenditures											
Expensing of exploration and development costs and percentage over cost depletion: oil and gas	2.0	4.9	3.4	0.1	0.3	0.8	0.9	1.0	2.2	1.6	1.2
Unconventional fuel production credit (Section 29 credit)			-i-	-i-	0.8	1.3	1.5	1.2	4.5	0.1	-i-
Tax credit for electricity produced from renewable resources			-i-			-i-	0.1	0.3	1.1	1.3	1.4
Tax credits for alcohol fuels and biodiesel			-i-	-i-	-i-	-i-	-i-	-i-	0.1	6.5	0.1
Residential energy efficiency tax credits		0.5	0.8						0.3	0.4	1.9
Other	0.1	1.2	1.0	0.7	0.3	0.4	0.3	3.2	1.1	3.0	4.1
Total Energy Tax Expenditures	2.1	6.6	5.1	0.8	1.4	2.5	2.8	5.7	9.3	12.9	8.7
Excise Tax Credits											
Alcohol Fuels Credit		0.1	0.4	0.5	0.6	0.7	1.0	1.5	3.3	5.2	5.7
Biodiesel Producer Tax Credit										0.8	0.5
Grants in Lieu of Tax Credits											
Treasury Grant in Lieu of Tax Credit										1.1	4.2

Source: CRS calculations using JCT and OMB tax expenditure estimates.

Notes: Columns may not sum due to rounding. In cells containing "-i-" estimated tax expenditures were less than $50 million. Revenue loss estimates for excise tax credits are presented as reported by the OMB in the President's Budget. Excise tax revenue losses only reflect the estimated reduction in excise tax receipts, and not any federal income tax offsets.

Table A-2. Energy Tax Expenditures, Excise Tax Credits, and Grants in Lieu of Tax Credits: 2010 Dollars (billions of dollars)

	1977	1981	1985	1989	1993	1997	2001	2005	2007	2009	2010
Energy Tax Expenditures											
Expensing of exploration and development costs and percentage over cost depletion: oil and gas	6.0	10.5	6.0	0.2	0.4	1.0	1.1	1.1	2.3	1.6	1.2
Unconven-tional fuel production credit (Section 29 credit)			-i-	-i-	1.1	1.7	1.8	1.3	4.7	0.1	-i-
Tax credit for electricity produced from renewable resources			-i-			-i-	0.1	0.3	1.1	1.3	1.4
Tax credits for alcohol fuels and biodiesel			-i-	-i-	-i-	-i-	-i-	-i-	0.1	6.5	0.1
Residential energy efficiency tax credits		1.2	1.4						0.3	0.4	1.9
Other	0.2	2.5	1.7	1.1	0.4	0.5	0.4	3.6	1.1	3.0	4.1
Total Energy Tax Expenditures	6.2	14.2	9.2	1.3	2.0	3.3	3.4	6.3	9.3	13.0	8.7
Excise Tax Credits											
Alcohol Fuels Credit		0.1	0.7	0.8	0.8	0.9	1.2	1.7	3.5	5.2	5.7
Biodiesel Producer Tax Credit										0.8	0.5
Grants in Lieu of Tax Credits											
Treasury Grant in Lieu of Tax Credit										1.1	4.2

Source: CRS calculations using JCT and OMB tax expenditure estimates.

Notes: Columns may not sum due to rounding. In cells containing "-i- " estimated tax expenditures were less than $50 million. Values are adjusted to 2010 dollars using the OMB's GDP price index. Revenue loss estimates for excise tax credits are presented as reported by the OMB in the President's Budget. Excise tax revenue losses only reflect the estimated reduction in excise tax receipts, and not any federal income tax offsets.

Table A-3. Tax Expenditures for Fossil Fuels, Renewables, and Efficiency: 2010 Dollars (billions of dollars)

	1977	1981	1985	1989	1993	1997	2001	2005	2007	2009	2010
Fossil Fuels	6.20	10.65	6.36	0.64	1.56	2.75	3.18	2.78	7.42	2.62	2.40
Renewables		0.73	1.17	-i-	-i-	0.13	0.12	0.33	1.67	9.07	3.40
Efficiency		1.55	0.58			-i-	-i-	-i-	0.42	0.50	2.10
Fuels Excise Tax Preferences		0.12	0.68	0.78	0.80	0.88	1.21	1.67	3.47	6.02	6.17
Treasury 1603 Grants in Lieu of Tax Credits										1.06	4.21

Source: CRS calculations using JCT and OMB tax expenditure estimates.

Notes: In cells containing "-i- " estimated tax expenditures were less than $50 million. Values are adjusted to 2010 dollars using the OMB's GDP price index.

Appendix B. Cumulative Revenue Losses Associated with Various Tax Preferences

This appendix presents data on the revenue losses over time associated with various energy tax preferences. Specifically, the sections below present historical revenue losses associated with tax provisions that benefit the oil and gas sector, those that benefit renewable energy, and revenue losses associated with the excise tax credits for alcohol fuels.

Cumulative Revenue Losses: Oil and Gas Tax Preferences[53]

Over time, the primary tax incentives for oil and gas were the percentage depletion allowance and the ability to expense intangible drilling costs (IDCs). Before the 1980s, these were the only tax incentives designed specifically to promote investment in oil and gas. Tax preferences for oil and gas introduced in the 1980s and 1990s, such as expensing allowance for tertiary injectants and the tax credit for enhanced oil recovery, sought to encourage domestic production by providing tax incentives for difficult to extract domestic oil resources. **Table B-1** provides an estimate of the cumulative revenue losses associated with these tax provisions, through the year 2000, in constant 2000 dollars.[54]

Table B-1. Petroleum-Related Tax Incentives Through 2000 (billions of dollars)

Tax Incentive	Years Included	Revenue Loss in Constant Year 2000 Dollars
Excess of Percentage over Cost Depletion	1968 - 2000	$81.7
Expensing of IDCs	1968 - 2000	54.6
Credit for Enhanced Oil Recovery Costs	1994 - 2000	0.5
Expensing of Tertiary Injectants	1980 - 2000	0.3

Source: GAO

Notes: Revenue losses reported the sum of JCT's annual estimates, and were adjusted for inflation by GAO. The Treasury estimates that the value of the exemption from passive loss limits for oil and gas companies was worth $1.1 billion over the 1998 – 2000 time period. The JCT does not view the exemption from passive loss limits as a tax expenditure. Thus, it has not been included in this analysis.

Table B-2. Estimated Revenue Losses Associated with Oil and Gas Tax Preferences (billions of dollars)

Tax Incentive	2000-2009 (2009 Dollars)	2010
Excess of Percentage over Cost Depletion	7.9	0.5
Expensing of IDCs	8.4	0.7
Credit for Enhanced Oil Recovery Costs	1.8	-i-
Reduced G&G Amortization Period	0.2	0.1
Election to Expense 50% of Refinery Costs	0.9	0.7

Source: CRS calculations using annual JCT tax expenditure estimates.

Notes: Values are adjusted to 2009 dollars using the Office of Management and Budget (OMB)'s GDP price index. Years 2010 through 2014 are presented in current dollars. An -i- indicates positive revenue losses of less than $50 million dollars. Rows may not sum due to rounding. Oil and gas related tax expenditures with annual estimates of *de minimis* value (less than $50 million) are not presented in JCT's annual tax expenditure tables and thus not included. These include the expensing of tertiary injectants and the credit for production from marginal wells. The JCT does not classify exemptions to passive loss rules as a tax expenditure as the effects of the exemption are reflected in the value of related tax expenditures.

Table B-2 presents historical revenue losses over the 2000 through 2010 period. As was the case in the earlier time period referenced above, the percentage depletion allowance and ability to expense IDCs continues to make up the majority of oil and gas related federal revenue losses.

Table B-3. Cumulative Revenue Losses: 1968 - 2010 (billions of dollars)

Tax Incentive	Revenue Loss in Constant Year 2010 Dollars
Excess of Percentage over Cost Depletion	$111.0
Expensing of IDCs	77.7
Credit for Enhanced Oil Recovery Costs	2.4
Expensing of Tertiary Injectants	0.4
Reduced G&G Amortization Period	0.3
Election to Expense 50% of Refinery Costs	1.6
Total (Without Interaction Effects)	**193.4**

Source: CRS calculations using GAO and JCT data.

Notes: Values are adjusted to 2010 dollars using the Office of Management and Budget (OMB)'s GDP price index.

Cumulative revenue losses, combining the data from **Table B-1** and **Table B-2**, are presented in **Table B-3**. Since 1968, the percentage depletion allowance has resulted in an estimated $111 billion in federal revenue loss. The ability to expense IDCs has resulted in an estimated $78 billion over the same time period. The majority of historical revenue losses associated with targeted tax incentives for oil and gas are attributable to these two provisions. From 1968 through 2010, estimated revenue losses associated with targeted tax incentives for the oil and gas sector sum to $193.4 billion.[55]

Table B-4. Tax Expenditures for Renewable Energy: Current Dollars (billions of dollars)

Tax Incentive	1979-1989	1990-1999	2000-2009	2010	Total
Business					
Renewable Energy Investment Tax Credit (ITC)	1.9	0.2	0.1	(i)	2.2
Renewable Energy Production Tax Credit (PTC)		0.1	6.0	1.4	7.5
Accelerated Depreciation (5-year) for Renewable Energy Investments[a]			0.5	0.3	0.8
Clean Renewable Energy Bonds (CREBs)			(i)	0.1	0.1
Credit for Investment in Advanced Energy Property			0.1	0.5	0.6
Section 1603 Grants in Lieu of Tax Credits (outlays)			1.1	4.2	5.3
Residential					
Residential Energy Efficient Property Credit[b]	2.7		0.1	0.2	3.0
Total (Without Interaction Effects)	**4.6**	**0.3**	**7.9**	**6.7**	**19.4**

Source: CRS analysis of data from the JCT and Treasury.

Notes: Beginning in 1986, the JCT reported tax expenditure estimates in billions of dollars, rather than millions. Tax expenditures of less than $50 million were recorded as a de minimis value and are therefore not included in the analysis. A value of (i) indicates positive revenue loss estimate of less than $50 million.

a. Accelerated depreciation for investments in renewables was included in JCT's annual tax expenditure report for the first time in 2008. Although qualifying renewable investments have been eligible for five-year cost recovery since 1986, the JCT's annual tax expenditure report did not identify the provision as a tax expenditure prior to 2008.

b. In years 1979 and 1980, the JCT tax expenditure estimates for residential energy credits did not distinguish between incentives for conservation and those for renewable energy property. One-half of the reported tax expenditure for residential energy credits in 1979 and 1980 has been allocated to renewables and used in calculating the totals presented in the table.

Cumulative Revenue Losses: Renewables

Historically, the primary tax incentives for renewable energy have been the investment tax credit (ITC) and production tax credit (PTC). The ability to forgo these tax credits and instead receive a one-time grant from the Treasury under Section 1603 of ARRA substantially increased the cost of these provisions during recent years. **Table B-4** and **Table B-5** present historical data on tax expenditures for renewable energy.

Since tax incentives for renewable energy were first introduced in the late 1970s, the estimated cumulative cost has been $24.6 billion. Of this, $5.3 billion is due to outlay payments under the Section 1603 grants in lieu of tax credits program. An estimated $12.2 billion, roughly half of the total support through tax-related incentives, is attributable to the renewable energy ITC and PTC.

Table B-5. Tax Expenditures for Renewable Energy: Constant 2010 Dollars (billions of dollars)

Tax Incentive	1979-1989	1990-1999	2000-2009	2010	Total
Business					
Renewable Energy Investment Tax Credit (ITC)	3.9	0.3	0.1	(i)	4.3
Renewable Energy Production Tax Credit (PTC)		0.1	6.3	1.4	7.9
Accelerated Depreciation (5-year) for Renewable Energy Investments[a]			0.5	0.3	0.8
Clean Renewable Energy Bonds (CREBs)			(i)	0.1	0.1

Table B-5. (Continued)

Tax Incentive	1979-1989	1990-1999	2000-2009	2010	Total
Credit for Investment in Advanced Energy Property			0.1	0.5	0.6
Section 1603 Grants in Lieu of Tax Credits (outlays)			1.1	4.2	5.3
Residential					
Residential Energy Efficient Property Credit[b]	5.4		0.1	0.2	5.7
Total (Without Interaction Effects)	**9.3**	**0.4**	**8.2**	**6.7**	**24.6**

Source: CRS analysis of data from the JCT and Treasury.

Notes: Historical spending has been adjusted to constant 2010 dollars using the composite GDP deflator. Beginning in 1986, the JCT reported tax expenditure estimates in billions of dollars, rather than millions. Tax expenditures of less than $50 million were recorded as a de minimis value and are therefore not included in the analysis. A value of (i) indicates positive revenue loss estimate of less than $50 million.

a. Accelerated depreciation for investments in renewables was included in JCT's annual tax expenditure report for the first time in 2008. Although qualifying renewable investments have been eligible for five-year cost recovery since 1986, the JCT's annual tax expenditure report did not identify the provision as a tax expenditure prior to 2008.

b. In years 1979 and 1980, the JCT tax expenditure estimates for residential energy credits did not distinguish between incentives for conservation and those for renewable energy property. One-half of the reported tax expenditure for residential energy credits in 1979 and 1980 has been allocated to renewables and used in calculating the totals presented in the table.

Cumulative Revenue Losses: Excise Tax Credits for Alcohol Fuels

Table B-6 presents estimated revenue losses associated with the excise tax exemption for alcohol fuels from 1980 through 2010. The first row presents revenue losses in current dollars. The second row presents revenue losses in 2010 inflation-adjusted dollars. The third row presents estimated revenue losses adjusting for income tax offsets (discussed below), in 2010 inflation adjusted-dollars. Over time, federal revenue losses increased, reflecting increased use of alcohol fuels, particularly ethanol.

Table B-6. Alcohol Fuels Excise Tax Exemption: Estimated Revenue Losses (billions of dollars)

Tax Incentive	1980-1989	1990-1999	2000-2004	2005-2010	Total
Alcohol Fuels Excise Tax Benefits: Revenue Losses in Current Dollars	2.8	6.0	5.5	22.6	36.8
Alcohol Fuels Excise Tax Benefits: Revenue Losses in 2010 Inflation-Adjusted Dollars	5.1	8.6	6.7	23.4	43.8
Alcohol Fuels Excise Tax Benefits Including Income Tax Offsets: 2010 Inflation-Adjusted Dollars	5.1	8.6	6.7	29.3	49.7

Source: Revenue losses over each five-year period were calculated by CRS using Treasury tax expenditure data reported in the President's annual budget proposals.

Notes: For inflation-adjusted dollars, the Office of Management and Budget's (OMB) GDP price index is used to make adjustments. The Treasury reports estimated federal revenue losses associated with tax credits for all alcohol fuels. These revenue losses are primarily attributable to ethanol.

Beginning in 2005, the volumetric ethanol excise tax credit (VEETC) was introduced to replace the previously available excise tax exemption for ethanol. Since excise tax credits are deductible, replacing the excise tax exemption with an excise tax credit has additional federal revenue consequences, above and beyond payouts for the excise tax credit. Specifically, income tax receipts decrease due to the higher excise tax deduction. Assuming an average tax rate of 25%, excise tax credits resulting in \$5.7 billion in lost excise tax receipts in 2010 also reduce income tax receipts by an estimated \$1.4 billion (\$5.7 * 0.25). Between 2005 and 2010, income tax offsets (foregone income tax receipts) associated with the alcohol fuels excise tax credit can be approximated at \$5.7 billion (\$22.6 * 0.25). Including estimated income tax offsets, and adjusting for inflation, total federal losses associated with alcohol fuels excise tax credits between 2005 and 2010 were approximately \$29.3 billion dollars. Since the introduction of excise tax preferences for alcohol fuels, these excise incentives have resulted in \$43.8 billion in revenue losses. When including estimated revenue losses associated with income tax offsets, total revenue losses associated with excise tax preferences for alcohol fuels between 1980 and 2010 total an estimated \$49.7 billion.

End Notes

[1] An economically efficient distribution of energy resources can be thought of as one that maximizes energy production and efficiency at the lowest possible cost. When considering cost, all costs, including external costs such as externalities and national security concerns, should be taken into account.

[2] Tax expenditures are federal revenue losses (reduced governmental receipts) associated with tax provisions allowing for special exemptions, deductions, credits, income deferrals, or reduced rates.

[3] Qualifying fuels under the credit (often referred to as the "Section 29" credit) included oil produced from shale or tar sands, gas produced from geopressurized brine, Devonian shale, tight formations, or coalbed methane, gas from biomass, and synthetic fuels from coal.

[4] For additional background, see CRS Report R41635, *ARRA Section 1603 Grants in Lieu of Tax Credits for Renewable Energy: Overview, Analysis, and Policy Options*, by Phillip Brown and Molly F. Sherlock.

[5] Salvatore Lazzari, former CRS specialist, outlined these eras in previous CRS reports.

[6] For an overview of the current status of energy tax policy, see CRS Report R41769, *Energy Tax Policy: Issues in the 112th Congress*, by Molly F. Sherlock and Margot L. Crandall-Hollick.

[7] Intangible drilling costs (IDCs) include wages, machinery used for grading and drilling, and unsalvageable materials used in developing wells. Special tax provisions allow producers to expense (deduct immediately) IDCs. In the absence of this provision, non-capital expenses associated with oil exploration and drilling would be capitalized into the basis of the property and the costs allocated as income is earned from the well over time. Currently, independent oil producers can fully expense IDCs. Integrated oil companies can expense 70% of such costs and depreciate the remaining 30% over five years.

[8] Coal was allowed the percentage depletion deduction beginning in 1932.

[9] If oil and gas producers were subject to normal income tax treatment, expenses associated with developing energy and mineral properties would be capitalized into the basis of the property and recovered over time as output is produced. Under percentage depletion, producers can recover investment costs (other than IDCs that were already expensed) by claiming a depletion allowance that is a fixed percentage of gross receipts as opposed to a deduction for the actual value of the resource extracted. When first introduced, the percentage depletion rate was 27.5% for oil and gas. Currently, percentage depletion is allowed for independent producers at a rate of 15% for oil and gas and 10% for coal. Percentage depletion is allowed on production up to 1,000 barrels of average daily production of oil (or its equivalent for natural gas). The depletion allowance cannot exceed 100% of taxable income from the property (50% for coal) or 65% of the producers taxable income from all sources.

[10] The federal "gas guzzler" tax was introduced under the Energy Tax Act of 1978 (ETA78; P.L. 95-618). This tax imposes an excise tax on automobiles with low fuel economy ratings.

[11] The windfall profit tax (WPT80) was enacted in 1980 under the Crude Oil Windfall Profit Tax Act (P.L. 96-223). The windfall profit tax was an excise tax imposed on domestically produced crude oil. This tax was repealed in 1988.

[12] The environmental excise tax on crude oil received at a U.S. refinery was enacted under the Comprehensive, Environmental Response, Compensation, and Liability Act of 1980 (P.L. 96-510), also known as the "Superfund" program, was designed to charge oil refineries for the cost of releasing any hazardous materials that resulted from the refining of crude oil. This tax expired at the end of 1995. For more information see CRS Report R41039, *Comprehensive Environmental Response, Compensation, and Liability Act: A Summary of Superfund Cleanup Authorities and Related Provisions of the Act*, by David M. Bearden.

[13] Tax policy can be distortionary when firms and individuals change their behavior to avoid paying taxes or to take advantage of subsidies. Taxes distort markets to the extent that price

signals are altered, leading to too much (or too little) production or consumption. When consumers and producers are more responsive to price changes, price changes resulting from taxes lead to larger market distortions. Not all distortions are bad, as those that correct for externalities, such as taxes on polluting activities, may improve market outcomes.

[14] The PTC was later expanded to include additional renewable energy sources, including geothermal, solar, open-loop biomass, small irrigation power, landfill gas, and municipal solid waste.

[15] This tax would be a broad-based general tax primarily on oil, gas, and coal based on the Btu of heat output.

[16] Specifically, open-loop biomass, geothermal energy, solar energy, small irrigation power, landfill gas, and municipal solid waste combustion were added to the list of eligible technologies.

[17] Energy Information Administration, *Federal Financial Interventions and Subsidies in Energy Markets 2007*, U.S. Department of Energy, Washington, DC, April 2008.

[18] For a full explanation of the Energy Policy Act of 2005 see U.S. Congress, Joint Committee on Taxation, *General Explanation of Tax Legislation Enacted in the 109th Congress*, committee print, prepared by Joint Committee on Taxation, 109th Cong., January 17, 2007, JCS-1-00.

[19] For more information see CRS Report R40999, *Energy Tax Policy: Issues in the 111th Congress*, by Molly F. Sherlock and Donald J. Marples, and CRS Report R40412, *Energy Provisions in the American Recovery and Reinvestment Act of 2009 (P.L. 111-5)*, coordinated by Fred Sissine.

[20] For additional background, and information on energy tax provisions scheduled to expire at the end of 2011, see CRS Report R41769, *Energy Tax Policy: Issues in the 112th Congress*, by Molly F. Sherlock and Margot L. Crandall- Hollick.

[21] A more thorough discussion of the economic rationale for intervention in energy markets can be found in CRS Report R41769, *Energy Tax Policy: Issues in the 112th Congress*, by Molly F. Sherlock and Margot L. Crandall- Hollick.

[22] An externality is a spillover from an economic transaction to a third party, one not directly involved in the transaction itself. When externalities are present, markets fail to establish energy prices equal to the social marginal cost of supply. The result is a system where cost and/or price signals are inaccurate, such that the socially optimal level of output, or allocative efficiency, is not achieved. Imposing a tax (subsidy) equal to the value of costs (benefits) associated with the externality enhances economic efficiency.

[23] Gilbert E. Metcalf, "Using Tax Expenditures to Achieve Energy Policy Goals," *American Economic Review*, *vol. 98*, no. 2 (2008), 90-94.

[24] Distortionary taxes are those that lead firms or consumers to change their behavior. For example, if a tax on income is used to fund public transportation subsidies, this could lead to a reduction in income-generating activities, reducing economic output.

[25] *Ibid.*, pp. 90-94.

[26] See CRS Report R40670, *Energy Efficiency in Buildings: Critical Barriers and Congressional Policy*, by Paul W. Parfomak, Fred Sissine, and Eric A. Fischer.

[27] In 2008, 57% of the petroleum consumed in the United States came from foreign sources. Of the imported petroleum, 45% came from the western hemisphere, 22% from Africa, 21% from the Persian Gulf, and 12% from other locations. U.S. Energy Information Administration, available at http://tonto.eia.doe.gov/energyexplained/index.cfm?page=oil_imports.

[28] For a review of the literature on the cost to the U.S. government of security related to foreign oil, see Keith Crane, Andreas Goldthau, and Michael Toman, et al., *Imported Oil and U.S. National Security* (Arlington , VA: RAND Corporation, 2009), pp. 59-74.

[29] For information regarding the differences in the tax expenditures provided by the Treasury and those provided by the JCT, and information on tax expenditures generally, see CRS Report RL33641, *Tax Expenditures: Trends and Critiques*, by Thomas L. Hungerford.

[30] An excise tax is generally levied on the production or sale of a specific good. Examples of excise taxes include those imposed on gasoline, tobacco, and alcohol.

[31] Tax expenditure estimates are taken from the annual JCT reports on tax expenditures. Since the JCT generally updates its tax expenditure estimates annually, annual estimates rather than five-year or 10-year estimates are used to generate the figures presented here.

[32] Rising incomes lead to an increase in the revenue losses associated with tax expenditures as individuals fall into higher income brackets and have a higher tax liability, making the value of deductions greater to the individual (more expensive in terms of revenue losses) and increasing the scope for claiming federal tax credits.

[33] Currently, mandates exist for renewable fuels and the federal government has considered mandates for renewable electricity. A full evaluation of non-tax energy policy programs is beyond the scope of this report.

[34] For details regarding why it is unknown whether a summation of individual tax provisions understates or overstates the federal revenue effect see CRS Report RL33641, *Tax Expenditures: Trends and Critiques*, by Thomas L. Hungerford.

[35] Martin A. Sullivan, "Multibillion Dollar Coal Credit: Lots of Form, Little Substance," *Tax Notes*, October 6, 2003, 34-43.

[36] Eric Toder, "Eliminating Tax Expenditures with Adverse Environmental Effects," *The Brookings Institution: Policy Brief*, July 2007.

[37] For additional background, see CRS Report R41635, *ARRA Section 1603 Grants in Lieu of Tax Credits for Renewable Energy: Overview, Analysis, and Policy Options*, by Phillip Brown and Molly F. Sherlock.

[38] The Treasury maintains a list of grant recipients. This list is available at http://www.treasury.gov/initiatives/recovery/ Pages/1603.aspx.

[39] Black liquor claimed this tax credit under IRC § 6426, which expired at the end of 2009.

[40] Martin A. Sullivan, "IRS Allows New $25 Billion Tax Break for Paper Industry," *Tax Notes*, October 19, 2009, pp. 271-272.

[41] Tax expenditures associated with the cellulosic biofuel producer credit are still expected to increase above historic levels as the renewable fuel standards (RFS) mandates additional use of cellulosic biofuels in the coming years. For background information, see CRS Report R40155, *Renewable Fuel Standard (RFS): Overview and Issues*, by Randy Schnepf and Brent D. Yacobucci.

[42] U.S. Congress, Joint Committee on Taxation, *Technical Explanation of the Revenue Provisions of the "Reconciliation Act of 2010," as Amended, in Combination with the "Patient Protection and Affordable Care Act,"* committee print, 111th Cong., March 21, 2010, JCX-18-10, 140-141.

[43] The data presented in Figure 4 only include expenditures that could be categorized as benefiting fossil fuels, renewables, or efficiency. Revenue losses from other energy tax provisions are not included in Figure 4.

[44] For additional background see CRS Report RL32979, *Alcohol Fuels Tax Incentives*, by Salvatore Lazzari.

[45] Allowing an excise tax credit, as opposed to an excise tax exemption, increases the value of the tax incentive to the taxpayer. Excise tax payments are deductible, and can be used to reduce taxable income. With an excise tax credit, the taxpayer first pays a higher excise tax rate and later receives a credit against excise tax paid. Since the taxpayer initially paid the higher excise tax rate, the taxpayers is able to deduct that higher excise tax as an expense to offset taxable income. With an excise tax exemption, the taxpayer is only able to deduct the reduced excise tax payment, rather than the full excise tax payment, from income before calculating income tax liability.

[46] The revenue losses associated with excise tax credits for alcohol fuels are presented as reductions in federal excise tax receipts. These estimates do not include income tax offsets. Since excise taxes are deductible against income, the actual federal revenue losses associated with excise tax credit will be greater than what is reported here.

[47] It is important to note that the magnitude of federal revenue losses does not address the relative subsidy provided to various sources of electricity or fuel. Effective tax rates may provide a useful tool for comparing the relative tax subsidization of various energy sources. For more information on effective tax rates for various energy sources see Gilbert E. Metcalf, *Taxing Energy in the United States: Which Fuels Does the Tax Code Favor*, The Center for Energy Policy and the Environment at the Manhattan Institute, January 2009.

[48] For additional information, see CRS Report R41635, *ARRA Section 1603 Grants in Lieu of Tax Credits for Renewable Energy: Overview, Analysis, and Policy Options*, by Phillip Brown and Molly F. Sherlock.

[49] The Department of the Treasury maintains a list of grant recipients. This list can be found at http://www.ustreas.gov/ recovery/1603.shtml.

[50] Tax expenditures categorized as those benefiting fossil fuels include the following: expensing of IDCs for oil and gas, percentage over cost depletion for oil and gas, the exception from passive loss limitation for working interests in oil and gas property, the credit for enhanced oil recovery costs, expensing of tertiary injectants, tax credits for investments in clean coal power generation facilities, the reduced amortization period for geological and geophysical expenditures associated with oil and gas exploration, the amortization of air pollution control facilities, the 15-year MACRS for natural gas distribution lines, the election to expense 50% of qualified property used to refine liquid fuels, the unconventional fuel production credit, and the capital gains treatment of royalties from coal.

[51] Tax expenditures categorized as those benefitting renewables include the following: income tax credits for alcohol fuels and biofuels, renewable energy investment tax credits (ITCs), renewable energy production tax credits (PTC), deductions and credits for clean-fuel vehicles and refueling property, tax credits for other clean and alternative technology vehicles, tax credits for residential energy efficient (renewable energy production) property, five-year MACRS for certain energy property, credits for holders of clean renewable energy bonds, and the credit for investment in advanced energy property.

[52] Tax expenditures categorized as those benefitting efficiency include the following: the exclusion from income of energy conservation subsidies provided by utilities, the tax credit for energy efficiency improvements to existing homes, the tax credit for the production of energy efficient appliances, credits to holders of qualified energy conservation bonds, deduction for expenditures on energy efficient commercial building property, and other residential energy conservation (efficiency) incentives.

[53] For more information, see CRS Congressional Distribution Memoranda, February 3, 2011, Historical Revenue Losses Associated with Tax Incentives for Oil and Gas, by Molly F. Sherlock.

[54] These figures can be found in U.S. General Accounting Office, *Petroleum and Ethanol Fuels: Tax Incentives and Related GAO Work*, GAO/RCED-00-301R, September 25, 2000, pp. 1-25, http://www.gao.gov/new.items/ rc00301r.pdf. Data on tax expenditures prior to 1968 are limited, as annual tax expenditures were not regularly provided by both the JCT and Treasury prior to this date. Thus, data on historical revenue losses do not extend back beyond 1968.

[55] The oil and gas sector also benefits from a number of tax incentives that are more widely available, such as the production activities deduction (IRC § 199), certain foreign tax credit rules for dual-capacity multinational taxpayers, and the ability to use last-in, first-out (LIFO) inventory accounting methods. Since these preferences are not specific to the oil and gas sector, annual tax expenditure estimates do not provide data on annual revenue losses associated with these provisions attributable to the oil and gas sector.

In: Energy Taxes
Editor: Nathan Videt

ISBN: 978-1-62948-552-2

Chapter 2

ENERGY TAX POLICY: ISSUES IN THE 113TH CONGRESS*

Molly F. Sherlock

SUMMARY

The scheduled expiration of a number of energy tax incentives means energy tax policy will likely be considered by the 113th Congress. Under current law, for example, renewable energy projects that begin construction after the end of 2013 will not qualify for the renewable energy production tax credit (PTC). A number of other energy tax incentives, including provisions to support building energy efficiency and renewable fuels, are also scheduled to expire at the end of 2013. In the past, expired and expiring energy tax provisions have been extended as part of "tax extender" legislation.

Energy tax policy may also be considered as part of comprehensive tax reform legislation in the 113th Congress. A base-broadening approach to tax reform might consider the elimination of various energy tax expenditures in conjunction with a reduction in overall tax rates. Alternative revenue sources, such as a carbon tax, may also be evaluated as part of the tax reform process.

The President's FY2014 budget proposes a number of changes to energy tax policy. The Obama Administration proposes to repeal a number of existing tax incentives for fossil fuels, while providing new or expanded incentives for

* This is an edited, reformatted and augmented version of a Congressional Research Service publication, CRS Report for Congress R43206, dated September 4, 2013.

alternative and advanced technology vehicles, renewable electricity, energy efficiency, and advanced energy manufacturing.

Energy tax policy involves the use of one of the government's main fiscal instruments, taxes (both as an incentive and as a disincentive) to alter the allocation or configuration of energy resources and their use. In theory, energy taxes and subsidies, like tax policy instruments in general, are intended either to correct a problem or distortion in the energy markets or to achieve some economic (efficiency, equity, or even macroeconomic) objective. The economic rationale for government intervention in energy markets is commonly based on the government's perceived ability to correct for market failures. Market failures, such as externalities, principal-agent problems, and informational asymmetries, result in an economically inefficient allocation of resources—in which society does not maximize well-being. To correct for these market failures governments can utilize several policy options, including taxes, subsidies, and regulation, in an effort to achieve policy goals. In practice, energy tax policy in the United States is made in a political setting, determined by fiscal dictates and the views and interests of the key players in this setting, including policymakers, special interest groups, and academic scholars. As a result, enacted tax policy embodies compromises between economic and political goals, which could either mitigate or compound existing distortions.

INTRODUCTION

Energy tax policy involves the use of one of the government's main fiscal instruments, taxes (both as an incentive and as a disincentive) to alter the allocation or configuration of energy resources and their use. In theory, energy taxes and subsidies, like tax policy instruments in general, are intended either to correct a problem or distortion in the energy markets or to achieve some economic (efficiency, equity, or macroeconomic) objective. In practice, however, energy tax policy in the United States is made in a political setting, determined by fiscal dictates and the views and interests of the key players in this setting, including policymakers, special interest groups, and academic scholars. As a result, enacted tax policy embodies compromises between economic and political goals, which could either mitigate or compound existing distortions.

U.S energy tax policy as it presently stands aims to address concerns regarding the environment as well as those surrounding national security.

Incentives promoting renewable energy production, energy efficiency and conservation, and alternative technology vehicles address both environmental and national security concerns. Tax incentives for the domestic production of fossil fuels also promote energy security by attempting to reduce the nation's reliance on imported energy sources.

The idea of applying tax policy instruments to energy markets is not new. Until the 1970s, however, energy tax policy had been little used, except to promote domestic fossil fuel production. Recurrent energy-related problems since the 1970s—oil embargoes, oil price and supply shocks, wide petroleum price variations and price spikes, large geographical price disparities, tight energy supplies, and rising oil import dependence, as well as increased concern for the environment—have caused policymakers to look toward energy taxes and subsidies with greater frequency. The direction of U.S. energy tax policy has changed several times since the 1970s.[1]

During the first session of the 113th Congress, energy tax policy appears to be designed to encourage energy efficiency and renewable energy production while continuing to promote U.S. energy security.[2] However, in recent years, major tax-related incentives supporting renewable energy production have expired, with many of the remaining renewable energy and energy efficiency incentives set to expire at the end of 2013.[3] In the past, many of these incentives have regularly been extended by Congress, in some cases retroactively. Absent legislative action, renewable electricity projects that begin construction after December 31, 2013, will not qualify for the production tax credit (PTC). Also scheduled to expire at the end of 2013 are several incentives designed to promote energy efficiency, as well as several incentives that promote alternative fuels and biofuels. Many energy tax incentives that had expired at the end of 2011 or 2012 were temporarily extended as part of the American Taxpayer Relief Act (ATRA; P.L. 112-240) in the 112th Congress.[4]

The President's FY2014 budget contains proposals that would scale back existing tax incentives for fossil fuels, enhance tax incentives for energy efficiency in commercial buildings, extend expired and expiring tax incentives for renewables, and use tax credits to promote advanced energy manufacturing.[5] Similar proposals appeared in the President's FY2012 and FY2013 budgets.

The tax writing committees in both houses of Congress are actively engaged in tax reform processes. The House Committee on Ways and Mean established 11 tax reform working groups, of which one was specifically tasked with examining energy tax issues. The Joint Committee on Taxation

(JCT) published findings from these working groups in a May 2013 report.[6] The Senate Committee on Finance released a series of options papers for tax reform. The Infrastructure, Energy, and Natural Resources options paper was released on April 25, 2013.[7]

The economic rationale for interventions in energy markets helps inform the debate surrounding energy tax policy. This report begins by providing background on the economic rationale for energy market interventions, highlighting various market failures. After identifying possible market failures in the production and consumption of energy, possible interventions are discussed. The report concludes with an analysis of the current status of energy tax policy.

The **Appendix** of this report provides a brief summary of energy tax legislation from the 108th through 112th Congresses that has shaped current energy tax policy.

POLICY INTERVENTION IN ENERGY MARKETS

The primary goal of taxes in the U.S. economy is to raise revenues. There are times, however, when tax policy can be used to achieve other goals. These include the use of tax policy as an economic stimulus or to achieve social objectives. Tax policy can also be used to correct for market failures (for example, the under- or over-supply of a good), which without intervention result in market inefficiencies. There are a number of market failures surrounding the production and consumption of energy. Tax policy, as it relates to energy, can be used to address these market failures.

Rationale for Intervention in Energy Markets

There are a variety of circumstances in which government intervention in energy markets may improve market outcomes. Generally, government intervention has the potential to improve market outcomes when there are likely to be market failures. Externalities represent one of the most important market failures in energy's production and consumption. Market failures in energy markets also arise from principal-agent problems and information failures. Concerns regarding national security are used as a rationale for intervention in energy markets as well.

Externalities

An externality is a spillover from an economic transaction to a third party, one not directly involved in the transaction itself. Externalities are often present in energy markets as both the production and consumption of energy often involve external costs (or benefits) not taken into account by those involved in the energy-related transaction. Instead, these externalities are imposed on an unaffiliated third party. In the presence of externalities, the market outcome will likely lead to an economically inefficient level of production or consumption.

When externalities are present, markets fail to establish energy prices equal to the full cost to society of supplying the good. The result is a system where price signals are inaccurate, such that the socially optimal level of output, or allocative efficiency, is not achieved. Economic theory suggests that a tax be imposed on activities associated with external costs, while activities associated with external benefits be subsidized—in order to equate the social and private marginal costs. These taxes or subsidies are intended to provide a more efficient allocation of resources.

Many energy production and consumption activities result in negative externalities, perhaps the most recognized being environmental damage. Air pollution results from mining activities as well as from the transportation, refining, and industrial and consumer use of oil, gas, and coal. Industrial activity can also produce effluents that contaminate water supplies and lead to other damages to the land. These environmental damages can lead to lung damage and a variety of other health problems. The use of fossil fuels, both in the production of energy (e.g., coal-fired power plants) and at the consumer level (e.g., using gasoline to power automobiles), and the associated greenhouse gas emissions are widely claimed to have contributed to global climate change.[8]

There may also be market failures associated with external benefits stemming from the process of learning-by-doing. Learning-by-doing refers to the tendency for production costs to decline with experience. As firms become more experienced in the manufacturing and use of energy-efficient technologies their knowledge may spill over to other firms without compensation. In energy markets, early adopters of energy-efficient technologies and practices may not be fully compensated for the value of the knowledge they generate.[9]

Principal-Agent and Informational Inefficiencies

Market failures in energy use may also arise due to the principal-agent problem.[10] Generally, the principal-agent problem exists when one party, the agent, undertakes activities on the behalf of another party, the principal. When the incentives of the agent differ from those of the principal, the agent's activities are not undertaken in a way that is consistent with the principal's best interest. The result is an inefficient outcome. In energy markets, the principal-agent problem commonly arises when one party is responsible for making equipment purchasing choices while another party is responsible for paying the energy costs, which are related to the efficiency level of the purchased equipment.

For residential rental properties, the incentives for the landlords and tenants surrounding the adoption of energy-savings practices are often not aligned, demonstrating the principal-agent problem. Landlords will tend to under-invest in energy-saving technologies for rental housing when the benefits from such investments accrue to tenants (i.e., tenants are responsible for paying their own utilities) and the landlord does not believe the costs of installing energy-saving devices can be recouped via higher rents. Tenants do not have an incentive to invest in energy-savings technologies in rental units when their expected tenure in a specific property is relatively short, and they will not have enough time to reap the full benefits of the energy-conserving investments. There is also evidence that when utilities are included in the rent, tenants do not engage in energy-conserving behaviors. On the other hand, when tenants pay utilities on their own, energy- saving practices are more frequently adopted.[11] The implication is that inefficient energy use by tenants in apartments where utilities are included as part of the rent would offset energy-saving investments made by landlords; consequently, landlords under-invest in energy efficiency. In general, the under-investment in energy conservation measures in rental housing provides economic rationale for intervention.

In another example, the incentives of homebuilders and homebuyers may not be aligned. Consequently, the principal-agent problem may result in an inefficient utilization of energy- efficient products in newly constructed homes. Homebuilders may have an incentive to install relatively low-efficiency products to keep the cost of construction down, if they do not believe that the cost of installing energy-efficient products will be recovered upon sale of the property. The value of installing energy-efficient devices may not be recoverable, if builders are not able to effectively communicate the value of energy-efficient devices once installed. Further, since homebuilders are not able to observe the energy use level of prospective buyers they may not be able to choose the products that best match the use patterns of the ultimate energy consumer. The result may be less energy efficiency in new homes.

There are also informational problems that may lead to underinvestment in energy-efficient technologies. For example, homeowners may not know the precise payback or rate of return of a specific energy-efficient device. This may explain the so-called "energy paradox"—the empirical observation that consumers require an abnormally high rate of return to undertake energy-efficiency investments.[12]

National Security

Preserving national security is another often-cited rationale for intervention in energy markets. Roughly 40% of the petroleum consumed in the United States is derived from foreign sources.[13] There are potentially a number of external costs associated with petroleum importation, especially when imported from unstable countries and regions. First, a high level of reliance on imported oil may contribute to a weakened system of national defense or contribute to military vulnerability in the event of an oil embargo or other supply disruption. Second, there are costs to allocating more resources to national defense than necessary when relying on high levels of imported oil. Specifically, there is an opportunity cost associated with resources allocated to national defense, as such resources are not available for other domestic policy initiatives and programs. To the extent that petroleum importers fail to take these external costs into account, there is market failure.

In addition, the economic well-being and economic security of the nation depends on having stable energy sources. There are economic costs associated with unstable energy supplies. Specifically, increasing unemployment and inflation may follow oil price spikes.[14]

Potential Interventions in Energy Markets

When there are negative externalities associated with an activity, correcting the economic distortion with a tax, if done correctly, can improve economic efficiency.[15] While such taxes are theoretically desirable, historically, such taxes have been politically unpopular. Conversely, when there are positive externalities associated with an activity, a subsidy can improve economic efficiency. The tax (subsidy) should be set equal to the monetary value of the damages (benefits) to third parties imposed by the activity.[16] The tax serves to increase the price of the activity, and reduce the equilibrium quantity of the activity, while a subsidy reduces the price, increasing the equilibrium quantity of the activity.

The production and consumption of fossil fuel energy can have negative externalities via detrimental environmental impacts. While multiple policy options to address this externality exist, economists tend to favor an emissions tax to address this externality because of such a tax's efficiency advantage.[17] In the late 2000s, proponents of greenhouse gas controls favored a cap and trade policy, as proposed in House-passed American Clean Energy and Security Act of 2009 (H.R. 2454). The policy discussion in the 113th Congress, however, has shifted to focus on a carbon tax approach.[18]

An alternative approach to reducing the use of fossil fuels has been to subsidize energy production from alternative energy sources. There are concerns, however, that using subsidies to stimulate demand for alternative fuels, as an alternative to fossil fuels, may not be economically efficient. First, subsidies reduce the average cost of energy, and as the average cost of energy falls, the quantity of energy demanded increases, countering energy conservation initiatives.[19]

Second, while the subsidy is intended to enhance economic efficiency, subsidies may be inefficient to the extent they are funded with distortionary taxes.[20] Hence, the more economically efficient alternative may be to place a tax on the undesirable activity.

Other energy-related activities may have positive externalities. There is the potential for learning- by-doing from early adopters of energy-efficient technologies, indicating that there may be positive external effects associated with these activities. For this reason, subsidies given to early adopters may enhance economic efficiency. Further, positive externalities are associated with R&D activities that lead directly to technological innovations.[21] In addition to budgeted spending on R&D, the tax code provides incentives for firms to engage in energy R&D (for example, the energy research credit (Internal Revenue Code (IRC) § 41)).[22]

When principal-agent problems lead to a market failure, economically efficient corrective measures would be those that increase the equilibrium quantity of the underprovided good. The market for energy efficient technologies is one example of this type of market failure. Currently, a taxpayer's gross income excludes any subsidy provided by a public utility to a consumer for the purchase or installation of energy-saving devices (see IRC § 136). This exclusion subsidizes energy-efficient devices. This exclusion does not specifically target the inefficiency in rental housing created by the principal-agent problem, since the exclusion applies to both owner- and non-owner-occupied property. Nonetheless, the exclusion may serve to ameliorate some of the market failure in the provision of energy-efficiency for rental property.

There are also various options for market intervention to address the informational problem associated with energy consumption and energy-efficient technologies. One option would be an information-based solution, such as energy-efficiency labeling and education and awareness campaigns. Alternatively, a tax-incentive-based approach—such as a credit or deduction for the purchase of energy-efficient devices—could be used to address the market inefficiency. Given that this market failure is an informational problem, it might be more efficient to pursue information-based solutions (such as energy-efficiency labeling like the U.S. Environmental Protection Agency and Department of Energy's Energy Star program).

Finally, there are questions regarding the most efficient and effective mode of intervention to address the negative external costs, specifically national and economic security concerns, associated with the consumption of imported oil. One option would be to impose a tax to correct the distortion. There are two problems with imposing such a tax. First, a tax on imported oil is likely to violate trade agreements. This has led policymakers to pursue policies that subsidize domestic petroleum production.[23] The second problem is that oil is a commodity priced on world markets. The United States producing oil for its own use does not necessarily insulate consumers from global fluctuations in oil prices. Additionally, to the extent that oil price fluctuations impact export prices in other parts of the world, such as Europe and China, the United States is still likely to experience economic impacts from oil price fluctuations.[24]

Taxes as a User Charge

Energy taxes may be employed as user charges for a public good or a quasi-public good.[25] In the United States, non-toll highways and highway infrastructure have the public good property of non-excludability. Highways are not likely to be provided by the market because public goods and quasi-public goods are susceptible to the free-rider problem.[26] If the private market fails to provide a public good, like highways, then government intervention via provision of highways can enhance economic efficiency. The federal excise tax on gasoline is often viewed as a user fee for the federal highway system.[27] For the tax to be efficient and equitable, it would charge individuals in proportion to their benefit from the public good (the highway system). In practice, gas taxes do not reflect the cost to the user but instead depend on the fuel efficiency of a specific vehicle.[28] Furthermore, some of the revenues collected from the federal gas tax serve to subsidize public transportation, undermining the view of the federal gas tax as a highway user fee.

CURRENT STATUS OF U.S. ENERGY TAX POLICY

Current U.S. energy tax policy is a combination of long-standing provisions and relatively new incentives. Provisions supporting the oil and gas sector reflect desires for domestic energy production and energy security, long-standing cornerstones of U.S. energy policy. Incentives for renewable energy reflect the desire to have a diverse energy supply, also consistent with a desire for domestic energy security. Incentives for energy efficiency are designed to reduce use of energy from all energy sources. Incentives for renewable energy, energy efficiency, and alternative technology vehicles reflect environmental concerns. **Table 1** contains a current list of energy-related tax expenditures and other energy tax provisions.[29]

Fossil Fuels

There are a number of tax incentives currently available for energy production using fossil fuels. They can be broadly categorized as either enhancing capital cost recovery or subsidizing extraction of high-cost fossil fuels. Certain incentives are designed to support coal, while others tend to support the oil and gas sector. The fossil fuels related incentives listed in **Table 1** are estimated to reduce federal tax revenues by $20.6 billion between 2013 and 2017.

Among the capital cost subsidies, the allowance of the percentage depletion method is estimated to cost $6.7 billion between 2013 and 2017.[30] Under percentage depletion, a deduction equal to a fixed percentage of the revenue from the sale of a mineral is allowed. Total lifetime deductions, using this method, typically exceed the capital invested in the project. To the extent that percentage depletion deductions exceed project investment, percentage depletion becomes a production subsidy, instead of an investment subsidy.

Other capital cost recovery provisions include expensing of intangible drilling costs related to exploration and development and a decrease in the amortization period for certain geological and geophysical (G&G) expenditures.[31] The expensing of exploration and development costs is estimated to cost the federal government $6.7 billion in revenue losses over the 2013 through 2017 budget window, while the reduced amortization period for G&G expenditures is estimated to cost $0.7 billion over the same time period.

Compared to capital cost recover provisions, tax expenditures intended to offset high extraction costs are small. Credits for enhanced oil recovery and oil and gas production from marginal wells are currently phased out due to high oil prices, and thus are not expected to reduce federal revenues in the near term.[32] The expensing allowance for tertiary injectants is also estimated to cost less than $50 million over the 2013 through 2017 budget window.

There are coal-specific energy tax provisions. These include recently expired coal production credits, as well as tax credits to support the development of clean coal facilities.[33] The tax credits for investing in clean coal facilities are estimated to cost $1.2 billion over the 2013 through 2017 budget window.

Renewables

Several tax incentives subsidize the production of energy from renewable sources. While the specific incentives differ in design, they generally work to increase the after-tax return on an investment in renewable energy production by providing tax incentives on the condition of eligible investment or production. Between 2013 and 2017, the total cost of tax-related provisions supporting the production of renewable energy (tax expenditures and grants designed to replace tax expenditures) is estimated to be $39.6 billion. Of this total, $17.2 billion is for outlays under the Section 1603 grants in lieu of tax credits program. Thus, the cost of tax expenditure and excise tax incentives for renewables is estimated to be $22.4 billion between 2013 and 2017.

Table 1. Energy Tax Provisions (billions of dollars)

Tax Provision	Description	2013 Cost	2013 – 2017 Cost	Expiration Date	I.R.C. Section
Fossil Fuels					
Expensing of percentage over cost depletion	Firms that extract oil or gas are permitted to deduct 15% of gross income (up to 25% for marginal wells depending on oil prices; 10% for coal and lignite) to recover their capital investment in a mineral reserve. The amount deducted may not exceed 100% of net income in the case of oil and gas properties. Percentage depletion allowances for oil and gas property cannot exceed 65% of taxable income. The alternative to percentage depletion is cost depletion, where deductions are based on a taxpayer's adjusted basis in the property. Integrated oil and gas companies must use cost depletion.	$1.3	$6.7	none	611, 612, 613, 613A
Expensing of intangible drilling costs (IDCs) and development expenditures for hard minerals	Firms engaged in the exploration and development of oil, gas, or geothermal properties have the option of expensing (deducting in the year paid or incurred) rather than capitalizing (i.e., recovering such costs through depletion or depreciation) certain intangible drilling and development costs (IDCs). Integrated oil and gas companies can expense 70% of qualified IDCs, with the remaining 30% capitalized and amortized over a 60-month period. 70% of the costs paid or incurred for the development of a mine or other natural deposit (other than oil or gas) may be expensed.	$0.9	$6.7	none	616, 617, 263(c), 291

Tax Provision	Description	2013 Cost	2013 – 2017 Cost	Expiration Date	I.R.C. Section
Fossil Fuels					
Amortization of G&G expenditures associated with oil and gas exploration	Under the Modified Accelerated Cost Recovery System (MACRS), the cost of selected types of geological and geophysical (G&G) expenditures is depreciated over 2 years for independent producers and smaller integrated oil companies.	\$0.1	\$0.7	none	167(h)
Election to expense 50% of qualified property used to refine liquid fuels	A taxpayer may elect to expense 50% of the cost of any qualified property used for processing liquid fuel from crude oil or qualified fuels. The remainder is recovered using a 10-year recovery period under the modified accelerated cost recovery system (MACRS).	\$0.4	\$3.4	12/31/2013 (property must be under contract for construction by 1/1/10)	179C
Coal production credits	A \$6.59-per-ton production credit for refined coal used to produce steam, or a \$2.308 per-ton production credit for coal reserves owned by an Indian tribe (all adjusted for inflation from 1992).	(i)	\$0.2	12/31/2011 (refined coal excluding steel industry fuel) Property must be placed in service by 12/31/2008 – no credits paid after 12/31/2013 (Indian coal)	45
Credits for investing in clean coal facilities	Tax credit of 20% of investment for integrated gasification combined cycle (IGCC) systems and 15% for other advanced coal technology credit	\$0.2	\$1.2	volume limited (credits fully allocated)	48A, 48B

Table 1. (Continued)

Tax Provision	Description	2013 Cost	2013 – 2017 Cost	Expiration Date	I.R.C. Section
Fossil Fuels					
	allocations made under the Energy Policy Act of 2005 (P.L. 109-58). 30% credit for IGCC and other advanced coal technology credit allocations under the Energy Improvement and Extension Act of 2008 (P.L. 111-343).				
Amortization of air and pollution control facilities	Allows the pre-1976 5-year amortization period for investments in pollution control equipment for coal-fired electric generation plants available to those plants placed in service on or after January 1, 1976. The 5-year amortization incentive for pre-1976 plants applies only to pollution control equipment with a useful life of 15 years or less. In that case 100% of the cost can be amortized over five years. If the property or equipment has a useful life greater than 15 years, then the proportion of the costs that can be amortized over five years is less than 100%.	\$0.4	\$1.7	none	169 and 291
Renewables					
Credits for electricity production from renewable resources	Tax credit of 2.3¢/kWh for electricity produced from wind, closed-loop biomass, and geothermal energy. Tax credit of 1.1¢/kWh for electricity produced from open-loop biomass, solar, small irrigation, landfill gas, trash combustion, qualified hydropower, and marine and hydrokinetic sources.	\$1.7	\$9.7	12/31/2013 (construction start date)	45

Tax Provision	Description	2013 Cost	2013 – 2017 Cost	Expiration Date	I.R.C. Section
Renewables					
("PTC" or "production tax credit")	The tax credit is available for 10 years after the date the facility is placed in service. Taxpayers may also elect to receive a 30% ITC in lieu of the PTC.				
Energy credit ("ITC" or "investment tax credit")	Tax credit equal to 10% of investment in energy production using geothermal, microturbine, or combined heat and power methods. The tax credit is equal to 30% of investment in energy production using solar electric, solar hot water, fuel cell or small wind methods.	$0.5	$2.9	12/31/2016 (other technologies; solar has permanent 10% credit after 2016) none (geothermal excluding geothermal heat pumps)	48
Section 1603 grants in lieu of tax credits	Section 1603 allows taxpayers eligible for the PTC and ITC to receive a one-time cash grant in lieu of tax credits. Eligible facilities may qualify for a grant equal to 10% or 30%, depending on technology type, of a qualifying project's eligible cost basis.	$8.1[a]	$17.2[a]	12/31/2011 (construction start date)	45, 48
Residential energy-efficient property credit	Tax credit for 30% of the cost of the purchase of solar electric property, solar water heating property, geothermal heat pump property, or small wind energy property. Fuel cell power plants receive 30% credit, limited to $500 for each 0.5 kilowatt of capacity.	$0.9	$4.9	12/31/2016	25D

Table 1. (Continued)

Tax Provision	Description	2013 Cost	2013 – 2017 Cost	Expiration Date	I.R.C. Section
Renewables					
Five-year cost recovery of certain energy property	Accelerated depreciation allowances are provided under the modified accelerated cost recovery system (MARCs) for investments in certain energy property. Specifically, certain solar, wind, geothermal, fuel cell, and biomass property has a five year recovery period. Second-generation biofuel plant property is allowed an additional first-year depreciation deduction equal to 50% of the property's adjusted basis.	\$0.3	\$1.5	12/31/2013 (placed in service date for second-generation biofuel property) None (other technologies)	168
Credits for holders of clean renewable energy bonds	Provides a tax credit for the holder of the bond against its income tax. Clean Renewable Energy Bonds ("CREBs") are subject to a volume cap of \$1.2 billion with a credit rate set to allow the bond to be issued at par and without interest. New Clean Renewable Energy Bonds ("New CREBs") are subject to a volume cap of \$2.4 billion with a credit rate set at 70% of what would permit the bond to be issued at par and without interest.	(i)	\$0.5	volume limited (fully allocated)	54, 54C
Credit for biodiesel, renewable diesel, second-generation (cellulosic) biofuels,	\$1 per gallon for biodiesel, agri-biodiesel, and renewable diesel (extra 10¢ for small producers of agri-biodiesel). Alternative fuels (liquefied petroleum gas, P Series Fuels, compressed of liquefied natural gas, liquefied hydrogen, liquid fuel derived from coal using the Fischer-Tropsch process, compressed or liquefied gas or liquid fuel	\$2.2[b]	\$2.6[b]	12/31/2013 (second-generation biofuel) 12/31/2013 (biodiesel, renewable diesel,	40, 40A, 6426, 6427

Tax Provision	Description	2013 Cost	2013 – 2017 Cost	Expiration Date	I.R.C. Section
Renewables					
and alternative fuels	from biomass) qualify for a credit of 50¢ per gallon. Second-generation biofuel qualify for a credit of $1.01 per gallon. Depending on the specific incentive, tax credits go to fuel producers and/or blenders. Credits are generally coordinated income and excise tax credits.			and alternative fuels) 9/30/2014 for liquefied hydrogen	
Advanced energy manufacturing tax credit	30% tax credit for qualified investments in advanced energy property. A total of $2.3 billion was allocated for advanced energy property investment tax credits, which were competitively awarded by the Department of Energy (DOE) and the Treasury.	$0.3	$1.5	Allocation limit	48C
Energy Efficiency					
Credit for nonbusiness energy property	Tax credit for 10% of the amount paid for qualified energy-efficiency improvements and expenditures for residential energy property including qualifying improvements to the building's envelope, the HVAC system, furnaces, or boilers. Credit limited to $500 (limit applies to multiple tax years).	$3.0	$5.5	12/31/2013	25C
Deduction for expenditures on energy-efficient commercial property	Tax deduction for the cost of building envelope components, heating and cooling systems, and lighting. The deduction is limited to $1.80 per square foot for multiple improvements, or $0.60 per square foot for deductions with respect to certain subsystems.	$0.2	$1.1	12/31/2013	179D

Table 1. (Continued)

Tax Provision	Description	2013 Cost	2013 – 2017 Cost	Expiration Date	I.R.C. Section
Energy Efficiency					
Exclusion of energy conservation subsidies provided by public utilities	Subsidies are not taxable as income.	(i)	$0.1	none	136
Energy-efficient new home credit	Manufacturers of manufactured homes may claim $1,000 credit for building homes 30% more efficient than the standard; Contractors may claim $2,000 credit for building homes 50% more efficient than the standard.	(i)	$0.1	12/31/2013	45L
Credit for producing energy-efficient appliances	Tax credit based on energy efficiency. Maximum credit is $75 for dishwashers, $200 for refrigerators, and $225 for clothes washers.	$0.2	$0.6	12/31/2013	45M
Qualified energy conservation bonds	The Federal government has authorized the issue of $3.2 billion in Qualified Energy Conservation Bonds ("QECBs"). QECBs provide a tax credit worth 70% of the tax credit bond rate stipulated by the Secretary of the Treasury. QEC bonds issued by state and local governments must fund an energy-savings project, such as the green renovation of a public building, R&D in alternative fuels, and public transportation projects.	(i)	$0.3	volume limited (allocated to the States)	54D

Tax Provision	Description	2013 Cost	2013 – 2017 Cost	Expiration Date	I.R.C. Section
Alternative Technology Vehicles					
Plug-in electric vehicles and other alternative fuel vehicles	Credits available for plug-in electric vehicles are available up to $7,500 depending on kilowatt hour capacity of vehicle (prior to 2010 the credit limit was higher, up to $15,000 for qualifying heavy vehicles). Fuel cell vehicles receive a base credit of $4,000 for vehicles weighing less than 8,500 pounds. Heavier vehicles qualify for up to a $40,000 credit. An additional credit of up to $4,000 is available for cars and light trucks that exceed the 2002 base fuel economy. A 10% credit, up to $2,500, is available for the cost of electric-drive low-speed neighborhood vehicle, motorcycle and three-wheeled vehicles.	$0.4	$3.3	Plug-in electric vehicle credit volume capped (200,000) per manufacturer 12/31/2014 for fuel cell vehicles 12/31/2013 for electric drive low speed vehicles	30, 30B, 30D
Credits for alternative fuel vehicle refueling property	Qualifying property dispenses alternative fuels, including ethanol, biodiesel, natural gas, hydrogen, and electricity. A 30% credit for qualifying property, capped at $30,000 for business property and $1,000 for nonbusiness property.	(i)	$0.3	12/31/2013 (12/31/14 for hydrogen refueling property)	30C
Other					
Exceptions for energy-related publicly traded partnerships	Publicly traded partnerships are generally treated as corporations. The exception from this rule occurs if at least 90 percent of its gross income is derived from interest, dividends, real property rents, or certain other types of qualifying income.	$1.2	$6.7	none	7704, 851

Table 1. (Continued)

Tax Provision	Description	2013 Cost	2013 – 2017 Cost	Expiration Date	I.R.C. Section
Other					
	Qualifying income includes income derived from certain energy-related activities, such as fossil fuel or geothermal exploration, development, mining, production, refining, transportation, and marketing.				
Exclusion of interest on State and local government private activity bonds for energy production facilities	Exclusion of interest from private activity bonds used to finance privately owned or operated sewage, water, solid waste disposal, and heating and cooling facilities, certain private electric and gas facilities, hydroelectric dam enhancements, qualified green building and sustainable design projects from tax. Generally subject to private activity bond volume cap.	(i)	$0.3	none	141, 142
Depreciation recovery periods for energy specific items	Smart electric distribution property is allowed 10-year depreciation under the modified accelerated cost recovery system (MARCs). Certain electric transmission property is allowed 15-year depreciation. Natural gas distribution lines are also allowed 15-year depreciation.	$0.4	$2.6	various	168
Deferral of gains from the sale of electric transmission property	A taxpayer may elect to recognize the gain from the sale of certain electric transmission property over an eight year period.	$-0.2	$-0.6	12/31/2013	451(i)

Source: CRS compilation based on data from U.S. Congress, Joint Committee on Taxation, *Estimates of Federal Expenditures for Fiscal Years 2012–2017*, committee print, 113th Congress, February 1, 2013, JCS-1-13, U.S. Congress, Joint Committee on Taxation, *General Explanation of Tax Legislation Enacted in the 112th Congress*, committee print, February 2013, JCS-2-13, and the President's FY2014 budget, *Analytical Perspectives.*

Notes: Provisions estimated as *de minimis* (i.e., estimated to have a revenue loss of less than $50 million over the 2013 through 2017 period) are not included in **Table 1**.

(i) = less than $50 million per year for both individuals and corporations; (ii) = This figure includes the reduction in excise tax receipts for alcohol fuels, biodiesel, and alternative fuel mixtures.

a. These figures are estimated outlays under the Section 1603 grants in lieu of tax credits program.

b. These figures are the cost of extension as enacted as part of the American Taxpayer Relief Act (ATRA; P.L. 112-240).

Historically, the primary tax incentive for renewable electricity has been the production tax credit (PTC). The American Recovery and Reinvestment Act (ARRA; P.L. 111-5) substantially modified this incentive, allowing projects eligible for the renewable PTC or investment tax credit (ITC) to claim a one-time grant in lieu of the tax credits.[34] This grant was available for projects that were under construction before the end of 2011. Since grants will be paid out when facilities are placed in service, outlays will continue through 2017. Between 2013 and 2017, this provision is estimated to result in outlays of $17.2 billion. Since the grant is paid out at the start of a project, the cost of the grant program will be partially offset by reduced PTC claims over time.[35] Allowing investors to take a one-time grant instead of future tax credits is intended to address uncertainty renewable energy investors may have regarding their future tax positions. Since the grant program was allowed to expire at the end of 2011, new renewable energy projects are not eligible. Renewable energy projects, however, may still be eligible for the investment tax credit (ITC) or PTC, depending on the credit expiration date for various technologies.

Several other tax expenditures related to renewable energy have budgetary effects. First, there is the energy credit (sometimes called the investment tax credit (ITC)), which provides a credit equal to either 10% or 30% of eligible investment in renewable energy production. Second, there is the residential energy-efficient property credit, which provides a tax credit for the installation of renewable electricity generating property for a residential dwelling. Third, the reduced depreciable life for renewable energy investments provides an additional subsidy for businesses. Finally, while allocations are not currently available, subsidies for clean renewable energy bonds (CREBs) will continue to have a revenue cost over the 2013 through 2017 budget window.[36] Taken together, these four provisions are expected to result in $9.8 billion in federal revenue losses between 2013 and 2017.

Several income and excise tax credits are designed to support renewable and alternative fuels. Currently, biodiesel and renewable diesel, second generation biofuels, including cellulosic and algae-based biofuels, as well as a number of other alternative fuels qualify for tax credits. These credits are projected to cost $2.6 billion over the 2013 through 2017 budget window. However, under current law, tax credits for most biofuels and alternative fuels expire at the end of 2013. Extending these incentives beyond 2013 will increase their cost. Through 2011, alcohol fuels (including ethanol) were eligible for a $0.45 per gallon tax credit. Tax credits for alcohol fuels were allowed to expire at the end of 2011.

ARRA also provided $2.3 billion in tax credits for advanced energy manufacturing. Most of these tax credits were allocated to projects in 2009, although $150 million was available for a second allocation round in 2013. The federal government is expected to realize revenue losses as investors that were awarded these tax credits make qualifying investments over time. Between 2013 through 2017 period, revenue losses associated with this provision are estimated to be $1.5 billion.

Energy Efficiency

Incentives for energy efficiency and conservation primarily operate by providing incentives to owners of residential and commercial property that undertake energy-efficient upgrades. There are also incentives for manufacturers of certain energy-efficient products and for the issuance of qualified energy conservation bonds (QECBs). Between 2013 and 2017, the total cost of tax expenditures related to energy conservation is estimated to be $7.7 billion.

The majority of revenue loss from tax expenditures related to energy conservation is attributable to three incentives for property owners to undertake energy-efficiency improvements on existing buildings. Certain residential energy-efficiency improvements made during 2013 may qualify for a 10% tax credit of up to $500. Energy-efficient improvements for commercial property, including upgrades to a building's envelope, heating and cooling, or lighting system are eligible for a tax deduction, limited to $1.80 per square foot. Incentives for both residential and commercial energy efficiency are scheduled to expire in 2013. The exclusion from income of subsidies provided by utility companies to energy consumers undertaking energy-efficiency upgrades increases the value of such subsidies, encouraging individuals to undertake such improvements. Taken together, these three incentives for building energy efficiency are projected to cost $6.7 billion between 2013 and 2017. Extending tax incentives for residential and commercial energy efficiency beyond their scheduled expiration will increase projected revenue costs.

Manufacturers of energy-efficient new homes and energy-efficient appliances may also be eligible for tax incentives. These incentives are also scheduled to expire at the end of 2013. The cost of these incentives between 2013 and 2017 is estimated to be $0.7 billion. The projected cost of manufacturer incentives for energy efficiency will increase if these provisions are extended beyond their 2013 scheduled expiration.

Qualified energy conservation bonds (QECBs) also encourage energy conservation, by providing subsidized financing to energy conservation projects and other renewable energy projects.[37] All available QECB funds have been allocated to the states, with states responsible for making sub- allocations and selecting qualifying projects.[38]

Alternative Technology Vehicles

Currently, the primary tax incentive for alternative technology vehicles is the up to $7,500 tax credit for plug-in electric vehicles. [39] The credit will begin to phase out for each manufacturer once 200,000 qualifying vehicles have been sold.[40] In addition, since 2006, the tax code has at times provided incentives for other alternative technology vehicles. Vehicles eligible for tax incentives have included qualified fuel cell vehicles, hybrid vehicles, advanced lean burn technology vehicles, and alternative fuel vehicles, with credit amounts varying by the specific technology and vehicle type. The tax credit for hybrid vehicles, advanced lean burn technology vehicles, and other alternative fuel vehicles expired at the end of 2010. The tax credit for qualified fuel cell vehicles is scheduled to expire at the end of 2014. Between 2011 and 2015, total tax expenditures related to hybrid, alternative technology, and plug-in electric vehicles is estimated to be $3.3 billion. Through the end of 2013 (2014 in the case of hydrogen property) taxpayers installing alternative fuel refueling property may qualify for a tax credit. The estimated cost of this incentive is $0.3 billion between 2013 and 2017.

Other Provisions

There are a number of other energy tax provisions that arguably do not fall under the fossil fuels, renewable energy, energy efficiency, or alternative technology vehicles categories. The largest of these incentives, in terms of revenue cost, is the special tax treatment for energy-related publicly traded partnerships, costing an estimated $6.7 billion between 2013 and 2017.[41] Special depreciation periods for certain energy property, other than renewable energy property, are estimated to cost $2.6 billion between 2013 and 2017.

Excluding interest from private activity bonds related to energy production is estimated to cost $0.3 billion between 2013 and 2017.

ENERGY TAX ISSUES IN THE 113TH CONGRESS

In the FY2014 budget, the Obama Administration proposes to eliminate certain tax incentives for fossil fuels, while expanding various incentives for energy efficiency, renewable energy, alternative energy manufacturing, and alternative technology vehicles. Similar proposals have appeared in previous Obama Administration budget proposals. The 113th Congress may also choose to consider extension of various energy tax incentives scheduled to expire at the end of 2013.

The President's FY2014 Budget Proposal

The President's FY2104 budget contains a number of energy-tax related proposals (see **Table 2**). Specifically, the budget proposes to provide $33.6 billion in new energy tax incentives between 2014 and 2023.[42] Most of this cost is attributable to a permanent extension of the renewable energy PTC. The proposal would also make the PTC refundable and available to solar energy technologies. The President's FY2014 budget also proposes new tax credits for advanced technology and alternative-fuel vehicles, an expanded deduction for energy-efficient commercial building property, and additional allocations of tax credits for advanced energy manufacturing.

The President's FY2014 budget also proposes to eliminate certain tax incentives that support fossil fuels (see **Table 2**).[43] Eliminating these incentives would raise an estimated $48.0 billion between 2013 and 2023. Amongst these provisions, repealing the Section 199 production activities deduction for fossil fuels would raise the most revenue, an estimated $19.9 billion between 2013 and 2023.[44] Under current law, this deduction is available for all domestic manufacturing activities. The President's FY2014 budget proposal would retain the Section 199 deduction for other manufacturing activities, but disallow the deduction for oil and gas as well as coal and other hard mineral fossil fuels. The President's FY2014 budget also proposes to repeal expensing of intangible drilling costs (IDCs), percentage depletion, and several other tax incentives for fossil fuels (as listed in **Table 2**).

Also included in the President's FY2014 budget proposal are several provisions that would affect the energy sector, but are not targeted specifically to energy. For example, the President's FY2014 budget proposes to repeal last-in, first-out (LIFO) inventory accounting methods. Repealing LIFO would increase tax liability for firms holding inventories that increase in value over time (e.g., oil). The President's FY2014 budget would also modify the tax treatment of dual-capacity taxpayers, a proposal that would affect oil and gas companies operating abroad.

The budget also proposes to modify several other environmental taxes. Specifically, the budget proposes to (1) increase the Oil Spill Liability Trust Fund (OSLTF) excise tax by one cent and expand the scope of the tax to include crudes produced from bituminous deposits and kerogen- rich rock;[45] (2) reinstate and extend the Superfund excise taxes, including a 9.7-cents-per-barrel excise tax on domestic crude oil and imported petroleum products and a tax on hazardous chemicals and imported materials used in the manufacture of hazardous chemicals, at a rate ranging from 22 cents to $4.87 per ton; and (3) reinstate the corporate environmental income tax, which would levy a 0.12% income tax on the amount by which corporate modified alternative minimum taxable income exceeds $2 million.[46] JCT estimates that the proposed modifications to the OSLTF excise tax would raise $1.9 billion between 2013 and 2023, with the Superfund excise tax proposals raising $8.2 billion and the Superfund environmental income tax raising $12.9 billion over the same budget window.[47]

Expiring Energy Tax Provisions

The American Recovery and Reinvestment Act (ARRA; P.L. 111-5) contained a number of provisions that increased tax incentives available for renewable energy and energy efficiency. Support for renewable energy and residential energy efficiency has been reduced with the subsequent expiration of the Section 1603 grants in lieu of tax credits, lack of additional allocations in advanced energy manufacturing tax credits, and reduced limits on tax incentives for residential energy efficiency under the nonbusiness energy property credits. Federal financial support for renewables and energy efficiency will continue to decline if various energy tax incentives are allowed to expire as scheduled at the end of 2013.

Table 2. Energy Tax Proposals in the President's FY2014 Budget (billions of dollars)

Description		Revenue Change Estimate
New or Extended Incentives		
Tax Credit for Production of Advanced Technology Vehicles	Replace the credit for plug-in electric vehicles with an expanded credit available to a wider range of advanced technology vehicles. Credit capped at $10,000. Credit would be available through December 31, 2020, with a phase down beginning in 2018.	-1.7
Tax Credit for Medium- and Heavy-Duty Alternative-Fuel Commercial Vehicles	Provide a tax credit for dedicated alternative-fuel vehicles weighing more than 14,000 pounds. Credit capped at $40,000. Credit would be available through December 31, 2019 with a 50% credit available in 2019.	-1.0
Tax Credit for Renewable Electricity Production (PTC)	Permanently extend the renewable energy PTC, make the credit refundable, and add solar facilities as qualifying property.	-24.7
Tax Deduction for Energy-Efficiency Commercial Building Property	Permanently extend and increase the maximum value of the energy-efficient commercial building property deduction to $3.00 per square foot, increase the partial deduction to $1.00 per square foot, and provide a deduction for taxpayers achieving certain energy savings targets. Provide a new deduction based on anticipated and realized energy efficiency savings.	-4.6
Tax Credit for Advanced Energy Manufacturing	Provide an additional $2.5 billion for advanced energy manufacturing tax credits.	-1.6
Incentives to be Repealed		
Credit for Enhanced Oil Recovery (EOR)	Repeal the investment tax credit for EOR projects.	—
Credit for Oil and Gas Production from Marginal Wells	Repeal the production tax credit for oil and gas from marginal wells.	—

Table 2. (Continued)

Description		Revenue Change Estimate
Expensing of Intangible Drilling Costs (IDCs)	Repeal expensing and 60-month amortization for capitalized IDCs. IDCs would instead be capitalized and costs recovered under generally applicable cost-recovery rules.	13.7
Deduction for Tertiary Injectants	Repeal the deduction for tertiary injectant expenses.	0.1
Exception to Passive Loss Limitation for Working Interest in Oil and Gas	Repeal the exception from the passive loss rules for working interest in oil and gas.	0.2
Percentage Depletion for Oil and Gas and Hard Mineral Fossil Fuels	Repeal percentage depletion for oil and gas and hard mineral fossil fuels. Taxpayers with adjusted basis in oil and gas or hard mineral fossil fuel property could claim cost depletion.	11.7
Domestic Manufacturing Deduction for Oil and Gas, Coal, and Other Hard Mineral Fossil Fuels	Modify the definition of manufacturing activities such that income from oil and gas, coal, and other hard mineral fossil fuel property does not qualify.	19.9
Reduced Amortization Period for Geological and Geophysical (G&G) Expenditures	Increase the amortization period from two to seven years for independent producers' oil and gas exploration G&G expenditures.	1.3
Expensing of Exploration and Development Costs for Coal	Repeal expensing, 60-month amortization, and 10-year amortization of exploration and development costs for coal and other hard-mineral fossil fuels. Costs would instead be capitalized and depreciated or depleted according to generally applicable rules.	0.6
Capital Gains Treatment for Coal Royalties	Tax coal and lignite royalties as ordinary income.	0.6

Source: Department of the Treasury, *General Explanations of the Administration's Fiscal Year 2014 Revenue Proposals*, Washington , DC, April 2013 and U.S. Congress, Joint Committee on Taxation, *Estimated Budget Effects of the Revenue Provisions Contained in the President's Fiscal Year 2014 Budget Proposal*, committee print, 113th Cong., May 10, 2013, JCX-11-13.

A list of energy tax incentives scheduled to expire at the end of 2013 can be found in **Table 3**.[48] Absent Congressional action, the PTC will not be available for renewable energy projects that begin construction after 2013. Also scheduled to expire are tax incentives for biodiesel, renewable diesel, second generation biofuels (including cellulosic biofuels), and various alternative fuels. Incentives for energy efficiency in both commercial and residential buildings, as well as incentives for manufacturers of energy-efficient appliances, are also scheduled to expire at the end of 2013. Most recently expiring tax incentives were extended as part of the American Taxpayer Relief Act (ATRA; P.L. 112-240).

Tax Reform

Energy tax policy may be addressed as part of a larger tax reform effort in the 113th Congress.[49] One of the 11 House Ways and Means committee tax reform working groups was tasked specifically with reviewing energy tax issues. Comments received by the working groups on energy tax policy were diverse in both scope and purpose.[50] Some comments suggested eliminating all or some energy tax expenditures. Other comments suggested a "technology neutral" approach to energy tax policy. Others suggested a carbon tax. A number of the comments were narrow in scope and specific to certain provisions.

The Senate Committee on Finance's *Infrastructure, Energy, and Natural Resources* options paper included a range of energy tax policies.[51] Options ranged from eliminating all or some subset of energy tax expenditures, enacting "technology neutral" incentives, expanding incentives for renewables and efficiency, enacting a carbon tax, and changing tax rules for master limited partnerships (MLPs) for the energy sector.

Selected Energy Tax Legislation[52]

Dozens of energy tax-related bills have been introduced as of the date of this report in the 113th Congress. This section briefly reviews selected legislation.

Table 3. Energy Tax Incentives Expiring in 2013 (billions of dollars)

Provision	10-Year Revenue Change from Temporary Extension in P.L. 112-240
Credit for Nonbusiness Energy Property	-2.4
Alternative Fuel Vehicle Refueling Property (Non-Hydrogen)	*
Credit for Two- or Three-Wheeled Plug-In Vehicles	*[a]
Second Generation (Formerly Cellulosic) Biofuel Producer Credit	-0.1
Incentives for Biodiesel and Renewable Diesel	-2.2
Renewable Energy Production Tax Credit (Construction Start Date and ITC in Lieu of PTC Option)	-12.2[b]
Credit for Production of Indian Coal	*
Credit for Construction for New Energy Efficient Homes	-0.2
Credit for Energy-Efficient Appliances	-0.7
Mine Rescue Team Training Credit	*
Special Depreciation Allowance for Second Generation Biofuel Plan Property	*
Placed-in-Service Date for Partial Expensing of Certain Refinery Property[c]	—
Energy-Efficient Commercial Building Deduction[d]	—
Election to Expense Advanced Mine Safety Equipment	**
Special Rule to Implement Electric Transmission Restructuring	**
Incentives for Alternative Fuel and Alternative Fuel Mixtures (Other than Liquefied Hydrogen)	-0.4

Source: U.S. Congress, Joint Committee on Taxation, *List of Expiring Federal Tax Provisions 2013 - 2023*, committee print, 113th Cong., January 11, 2013, JCX-3-13 and U.S. Congress, Joint Committee on Taxation, *General Explanation Of Tax Legislation Enacted In The 113th Congress*, committee print, 112th Cong., February 25, 2013, JCS-2-13.

Notes: A "*" indicates an estimated cost of less than $50 million between 2013 and 2022. A "**" indicates that the provision was extended at no revenue cost. A "—" indicates that the provision was not extended in P.L. 112-240.

a. Credits for electric motorcycles and three-wheeled vehicles were modified and extended, but not the credit for low-speed vehicles.
b. As part of ATRA, the expiration date for the renewable energy production tax credit (PTC) was modified such that facilities that were under construction but not yet placed in service by the end of 2013 would qualify. The option to claim the ITC in lieu of the PTC was not available prior to 2009.
c. To qualify for this incentive, a binding construction contract must have been in place by January 1, 2010.
d. This provision was extended for five years, through 2013, as part of the Emergency Economic Stabilization Act (P.L. 110-343).

Carbon Tax

A carbon tax as a policy option has received increased attention in the 113th Congress.[53] Legislative initiatives to enact a carbon tax include the following:

- The Climate Protection Act of 2013 (S. 332) would establish a carbon pollution fee starting at $20 per ton of CO_2, increasing by 5.6% per year for 10 years.
- The Waxman / Whitehouse discussion draft would establish a carbon pollution fee, starting in the range of $15 to $35 per ton of CO_2 emissions, increasing at an annual rate in the range of 2% - 8%.[54]

Initiatives opposing a carbon tax have also been put forward. These include the following:

- The No Carbon Tax Act of 2013 (H.R. 1486) prohibits the Secretary of the Treasury or the Environmental Protection Agency from implementing a carbon tax.
- H.Con.Res. 8 expresses the opposition of Congress to Federal efforts to establish a carbon tax on fuels for electricity and transportation.
- H.Con.Res. 24 and S.Con.Res. 4 express the sense of Congress that a carbon tax is not in the economic interest of the United States.
- S.Amdt. 261 to S.Con.Res. 8 would create a point of order against legislation that would create a Federal tax or fee on carbon emissions.

Interest in the carbon tax approach represents as a shift away from the cap-and-trade option which was more popular in past Congresses. During the 111th Congress the House passed the American Clean Energy and Security Act of

2009 (H.R. 2454) (Waxman/Markey) which would have established cap-and-trade programs.

Master Limited Partnerships

Growing interest in the option of allowing renewables to be taxed as master limited partnerships (MLPs) is reflected in the Master Limited Partnership Parity Act (S. 795 and H.R. 1696).[55] Allowing renewables to be taxed as MLPs could reduce financing costs for renewable energy, but it would also likely result in corporate tax base erosion.

Other

A number of other energy tax bills have been introduced in the 113th Congress. Some legislation would repeal various energy tax incentives using revenues to reduce the corporate tax rate (e.g., the Energy Freedom and Economic Prosperity Act (H.R. 259)). Other legislation would repeal some subset of energy tax expenditures, such as those available to certain oil and gas companies (e.g., the Close Big Oil Tax Loopholes Act of 2013 (S. 307)).

There has also been Congressional interest in ensuring that tar sands oil is subject to the Oil Spill Liability Trust Fund (OSLTF) excise tax. Provisions to this effect were included as a revenue offset in the Student Loan Affordability Act (S. 953).[56]

Appendix. Energy Tax Legislation in Past Congresses

This appendix describes legislation during the 108th through 112th Congresses that shaped current energy tax policy.

Enacted Legislation in the 108th and 109th Congresses

The Working Families Tax Relief Act of 2004 (P.L. 108-311)

Several energy tax incentives were extended as part of the Working Families Tax Relief Act of 2004, a $146 billion package of middle class and business tax breaks. This legislation, which was signed into law on October 4, 2004, retroactively extended four energy tax subsidies: the § 45 renewable energy production tax credit, suspension of the 100% net income limitation for the oil and gas percentage depletion allowance, the $4,000 tax credit for electric vehicles, and the deduction for clean fuel vehicles (which ranges from $2,000 to $50,000). The §45 tax credit and the suspension of the 100% net income limitation had each expired on January 1, 2004 but were retroactively extended through December 31, 2005. The electric vehicle credit and the clean- vehicle income tax deduction were in the process of being phased-out (phase-out had begun on January 1, 2004). The Working Families Tax Relief Act of 2004 suspended the phase-out— providing 100% of the tax breaks— through 2005. The tax breaks were resumed beginning on January 1, 2006, when only 25% of the tax break was available.

The American Jobs Creation Act of 2004 (P.L. 108-357)

The American Jobs Creation Act of 2004 was enacted on October 22, 2004. It included about $5 billion in energy tax incentives primarily targeted at renewable energy as well as alcohol and biofuels. In particular, the act created the production tax credit, eliminated reduced tax rates for most blended alcohol fuels, established the biodiesel fuel and small refiner tax credits, and allowed a credit for oil and gas produced from marginal wells.[57]

The Energy Policy Act of 2005 (P.L. 109-58)

The Energy Policy Act of 2005 was enacted on August 8, 2005. It included an estimated $9 billion, over five years, in tax incentives distributed among renewable energy, conservation, and traditional energy sources. Among the larger provisions of the act, in revenue cost terms, were the enactment of several alternative technology vehicle credits, enactment of three investment credits for clean coal, and the extension of the production tax credit.

The Tax Increase Prevention and Reconciliation Act (P.L. 109-222)

The Tax Increase Prevention and Reconciliation Act (P.L. 109-222) was enacted May 17, 2006. It reduced the value of the subsidy by raising the amortization period from two years to five years, still faster than the capitalization treatment before the 2005 act, but slower than the treatment under that act. The higher amortization period applies only to the major integrated oil companies—independent (unintegrated) oil companies may continue to amortize all geological and geophysical (G&G) costs over two years—and it applies to abandoned as well as successful properties. This change increased taxes on major integrated oil companies by an estimated $189 million over 10 years, effectively rescinding about 20% of the nearly

$1.1 billion 11-year tax for oil and gas production under the Energy Policy Act of 2005.

The Tax Relief and Health Care Act of 2006 (P.L. 109-432)

At the end of 2006, the 109th Congress enacted a tax extenders package that included extension of numerous renewable energy and excise tax provisions. Many of the renewable energy provisions in this bill had already been extended under the Energy Policy Act of 2005 and were not set to expire until the end of 2007 or later. The Tax Relief and Health Care Act of 2006 provided for one-year extensions of these provisions.

Enacted Legislation in the 110th and 111th Congresses

Energy tax policy in the 110th Congress represented a shift towards increased tax burden (via the removal of subsidies) on the oil and gas industry while also emphasizing energy conservation and alternative and renewable fuels, as opposed to conventional hydrocarbons.[58] This policy direction appeared to be the result of high crude oil and petroleum product prices and oil and gas industry profits, along with the political realignment of the Congress after the 2006 congressional elections. The shift was manifested by proposals to reduce oil and gas production incentives or subsidies, which were initially incorporated into, but ultimately dropped from comprehensive energy policy legislation. Later in the 110th Congress, enacted legislation focused on increasing incentives for renewable energy production, rather than reducing tax incentives available to the oil and gas industries. The fact that tax incentives for oil and gas were left in place is in part a reflection of the deteriorating business climate during 2008.

Energy tax legislation in the 111th Congress continued to provide additional support for renewables and energy efficiency. As was the case in previous Congresses, much of the energy tax legislation enacted during the 111th Congress extended expired or expiring energy-related tax incentives. The American Recovery and Reinvestment Act (ARRA; P.L. 111-5) introduced new incentives for renewable energy and advanced energy manufacturing, while providing enhanced incentives for residential energy efficiency. The 111th Congress also eliminated the "black liquor loophole."

Energy Independence and Security Act of 2007 (P.L. 110-140)

The Energy Independence and Security Act of 2007 (P.L. 110-140; H.R. 6) contained a number of provisions designed to increase energy efficiency and the availability of renewable energy. Specifically, the act increased the target fuel efficiency for combined fleets of cars and light trucks, increased renewable fuel standards, and increased a number of energy-efficiency standards for household and commercial appliance equipment.

Energy Tax Provisions in the Food, Conservation, and Energy Act of 2008 (P.L. 110-234)

The Food, Conservation, and Energy Act of 2008 (P.L. 110-234), otherwise referred to as the 2008 Farm Bill, contained two energy tax provisions.[59] The first provision promotes cellulosic biofuels through a production credit of $1.01 per gallon, which applies to fuels produced from qualifying cellulosic feedstocks. The second provision, the ethanol blender's tax credit (which applies to both domestic and foreign sourced ethanol), was reduced from $0.51 per gallon to $0.45 per gallon.[60]

The Emergency Economic Stabilization Act of 2008 (P.L. 110-343)

The Emergency Economic Stabilization Act of 2008 (P.L. 110-343), included $17 billion in energy tax incentives. These provisions were primarily extensions of existing provisions (extenders), but also including several new energy tax incentives. The new provisions included $10.9 billion in renewable energy tax incentives aimed at clean energy production, $2.6 billion in incentives targeted toward cleaner vehicles and fuels, and $3.5 billion in tax breaks to promote energy conservation and energy efficiency. The cost of the energy tax extenders legislation in the Emergency Economic Stabilization Act of 2008 was fully financed, or paid for, by raising taxes on the oil and gas industry (mostly by reducing oil and gas tax breaks) and by other tax increases.

The American Recovery and Reinvestment Act of 2009 (ARRA; P.L. 111-5)

ARRA modified incentives for renewable energy production, energy conservation, alternative technology vehicles, as well as a number of other energy tax incentives.[61] Collectively, ARRA's energy tax provisions lowered the cost of selected renewable energy relative to energy from other sources, such as oil and gas. Provisions enacted under ARRA extended and expanded a number of incentives for investment in renewable energy. The renewable energy production tax credit (PTC) was extended through 2012 for wind and 2013 for other eligible technologies, the energy credit (ITC) was expanded for small wind property, and taxpayers were given the option of receiving a direct grant from the Treasury in lieu of tax credits under the Section 1603 grant program.[62] Renewable energy production was also encouraged by ARRA's provision increasing the funds available for the issuance of new clean renewable energy bonds. Residential incentives for renewable energy property were expanded under ARRA, as property-specific credit caps for residential renewable energy property were removed.

ARRA contained two tax provisions intended to encourage energy conservation. The first provision modified the tax credits for energy-efficient improvements to existing homes by temporarily increasing the credit rate and removing credit caps previously associated with specific types of property. For qualified energy-efficiency improvements, such as the installation of energy-efficient building envelope components, furnaces, or boilers, installed during 2009 and 2010, taxpayers could claim a 30% tax credit.[63] ARRA also removed property-by-property caps on the tax credit and replaced them with a $1,500 cap for the total amount of the credit claimed during 2009 and 2010.[64] The second energy conservation provision increased funds available for the issue of qualified energy conservation bonds.

To further promote alternative technology vehicles, tax provisions enacted under ARRA modified the credits for alternative fuel vehicles and plug-in electric vehicles. Additionally, a tax credit for plug-in vehicle conversion was enacted.

Tax credits for advanced energy manufacturing (IRC § 48C) were also introduced under ARRA. This provision provided $2.3 billion in tax credits to be competitively awarded to qualifying projects.

The Health Care and Education Reconciliation Act of 2010 (P.L. 111-152)

Energy tax policy—like all tax policy—can lead to unanticipated consequences. Notably, this issue arose in the 111th Congress in its deliberations concerning "black liquor." In the context of taxes, the term "black liquor" referred to a process in which pulp mills use a mixture of conventional fuel and a byproduct of the pulping process as an energy source for the mill. According to changes enacted in The Safe, Accountable, Flexible, Efficient Transportation Equity Act: A Legacy for Users (P.L. 109-59; SAFETEA-LU), "black liquor" was eligible for the alternative fuels tax credit, which was not the congressional intent of the provision.[65] The IRS later ruled that black liquor would be eligible for the cellulosic biofuel producer credit after the alternative fuels mixture credit expired at the end of 2009.

Recognizing the unintended consequence, Senate Finance Committee Chairman Max Baucus[66] stated in response to draft legislation, "Our measure ensures this tax credit is used consistently as the law intended, not through an unintended loophole." Senator Charles Grassley[67] made similar statements, noting "The paper industry was not intended to receive the alternative fuels tax credit when the credit was enacted." Under The Health Care and Education Reconciliation Act of 2010 (P.L. 111-152), black liquor was made ineligible for the cellulosic biofuel producer credit, reducing revenue losses by $23.6 billion between 2011 and 2019.[68] In addition, with the passage of The Tax Relief, Unemployment Insurance Reauthorization and Job Creation Act of 2010 (P.L. 111-312) at the end of 2010, black liquor could no longer qualify for the alternative fuels tax credit. However, taxpayers may still be claiming tax credits for black liquor, as previously unused credits may be carried forward.

The Tax Relief, Unemployment Insurance Reauthorization, and Job Creation Act of 2010 (P.L. 111-312)

A number of expiring energy tax provisions were temporarily extended in the Tax Relief, Unemployment Reauthorization, and Job Creation Act of 2010 (P.L. 111-312). The one-year extension of tax credits for alcohol fuels, including ethanol, was estimated to cost $4.9 billion. Extending the Section 1603 grant in lieu of tax credits program for one year was estimated to cost $3.0 billion. The retroactive extension of tax incentives for biodiesel and renewable diesel, which had expired at the end of 2009, was estimated to cost $2.0 billion. Other provisions that were extended included tax credits for residential energy efficiency improvements,[69] energy efficient appliance manufacturers, and energy efficient new homes. Tax provisions related to refined coal, alternative fuel mixtures, electric transmission restructuring, percentage depletion for oil and gas production, and alternative fuel vehicle refueling property were also extended.

Enacted Legislation in the 112th Congress

Energy tax legislation enacted in the 112th Congress included measures to extend expired or expiring energy tax incentives. Notably, a number of energy provisions were not extended, including tax credits for ethanol and the Section

1603 grants in lieu of tax credits. Both of these provisions had expired at the end of 2011. The provision allowing for the suspension of the 100%-of-net-income limitation on percentage depletion, which had been part of multiple past tax extenders packages, was also not extended.

The American Taxpayer Relief Act of 2012 (P.L. 112-240)[70]

Several expired and expiring energy tax incentives were temporarily extended as part of the American Taxpayer Relief Act of 2012 (ATRA; P.L. 112-240). While most expiring energy tax provisions were simply extended through the end of 2013 under ATRA, substantive changes were made to the renewable energy production tax credit (PTC). Specifically, the expiration date for the PTC was changed from a placed-in-service deadline to a construction start date for all qualifying technologies. Extending the PTC for wind for one year and changing the deadline from a placed-in-service to construction start date was estimated to cost $12.2 billion over the 10-year budget window. Other provisions that were extended include credits for biodiesel, renewable diesel, alternative fuels, and second generation (cellulosic) biofuels. The tax credit for cellulosic biofuels was modified to include algae-based fuels. Other incentives related to energy efficiency, including the tax credit for nonbusiness energy property and the credit for the manufacture of energy-efficient appliances, were also extended.

End Notes

[1] For more, see CRS Report R41227, *Energy Tax Policy: Historical Perspectives on and Current Status of Energy Tax Expenditures*, by Molly F. Sherlock.

[2] For an overview of non-tax energy policy issues in the 113th Congress, see CRS Report R42756, *Energy Policy: 113th Congress Issues*, by Carl E. Behrens.

[3] See CRS Report R43124, *Tax Provisions Expiring in 2013 ("Tax Extenders")*, by Molly F. Sherlock.

[4] CRS Report R42894, *An Overview of the Tax Provisions in the American Taxpayer Relief Act of 2012*, by Margot L. Crandall-Hollick.

[5] Department of the Treasury, *General Explanations of the Administration's Fiscal Year 2014 Revenue Proposals*, Washington, DC, April 2013.

[6] U.S. Congress, Joint Committee on Taxation, *Report to the House Committee on Ways and Means on Present Law and Suggestions for Reform Submitted to the Tax Reform Working Groups*, committee print, 113th Cong., May 6, 2013, JCS-3-13.

[7] Senate Committee on Finance tax reform options papers can be found at http://www. finance. senate.gov/issue/?id= 6c61b1e9-7203-4af0-b356-357388612063.

[8] See CRS Report RL34266, *Climate Change: Science Highlights*, by Jane A. Leggett.

[9] Kenneth Gillingham, Richard G. Newell, and Karen Palmer, *Energy Efficiency Economics and Policy*, Resources for the Future, RFF DP 09-13, Washington, DC, April 2009.

[10] The extent of principal-agent problems in residential energy use is quantified in Scott Murtishaw and Jayant Sathaye, *Quantifying the Effect of the Principal-Agent Problem on U.S. Residential Energy Use*, Lawrence Berkeley National Labratory, August 12, 2006, http://www.escholarship.org/uc/item/6f14t11t.

[11] Arik Levinson and Scott Niemann, "Energy Use by Apartment Tenants when Landlords Pay for Utilities," *Resource and Energy Economics*, vol. 26 (2004), pp. 51-75.

[12] Gilbert E. Metcalf, "Using Tax Expenditures to Achieve Energy Policy Goals," *American Economic Review*, vol. 98, no. 2 (2008), pp. 90-94.

[13] While dependence on foreign oil has declined since 2005, about 40% of petroleum consumed in 2012 was imported. See Energy Information Administration, *How Dependent are we on Foreign Oil?*, May 10, 2013, http://www.eia.gov/ energy_in_brief/article/foreign_oil_ dependence.cfm.

[14] See James D. Hamilton, *Causes and Consequences of the Oil Shock of 2007-08*, National Bureau of Economic Research, Working Paper 15002, Cambridge, MA, May 2009. Hamilton evaluates the role of the oil shock of 2007- 2008 in the succeeding economic recession.

[15] There are non-tax options for addressing energy market failures such as regulation and private sector solutions. These options are beyond the scope of this report.

[16] Taxes imposed to correct for negative externalities are also known as Pigovian taxes, named after the economist who developed the concept, Arthur Cecil Pigou.

[17] CRS Report R40242, *Carbon Tax and Greenhouse Gas Control: Options and Considerations for Congress*, by Jonathan L. Ramseur and Larry Parker for a discussion of the relative merits and demerits of carbon taxes and cap-and- trade systems.

[18] See CRS Report R42731, *Carbon Tax: Deficit Reduction and Other Considerations*, by Jonathan L. Ramseur, Jane A. Leggett, and Molly F. Sherlock.

[19] Gilbert E. Metcalf, "Tax Policies for Low-Carbon Technologies," *National Tax Journal*, vol. 63, no. 3 (September 2009), pp. 519-533.

[20] Gilbert E. Metcalf, "Federal Tax Policy towards Energy," *Tax Policy and the Economy*, vol. 21 (2007), pp. 145-184.

[21] It should be noted that all R&D, not just R&D related to energy, is likely to have positive externalities. There is no reason to believe that energy R&D has positive externalities that differ from R&D in general, and hence no reason to believe that energy R&D deserves a differential subsidy.

[22] See CRS Report RL31181, *Research Tax Credit: Current Law and Policy Issues for the 113th Congress*, by Gary Guenther for an overview of the research tax credit, an umbrella credit under which the energy research credit falls.

[23] Subsidizing domestic production is also problematic in that such policies conflict with environmental objectives.

[24] Gilbert E. Metcalf, "Using Tax Expenditures to Achieve Energy Policy Goals," *American Economic Review*, vol. 98, no. 2 (2008), pp. 90-94.

[25] Public goods are those that are both non-rival (one person's consumption of the good does not diminish another's ability to consume that same good) and non-excludable (it is either impossible or prohibitively expensive to prevent consumption of the good once the good has been provided). Quasi-public goods are those that are either non-rival or non-excludable.

[26] The free-rider problem is the consequence of non-excludability. If all individuals are free to use a good once that good has been provided, no single individual has an incentive to be the provider of that good. Instead, the individual will wait for the good to be provided by another party. In the absence of government intervention, the market may fail to provide goods that are subject to the free-rider problem.

[27] For background information on the federal gas tax see CRS Report R40808, *The Role of Federal Gasoline Excise Taxes in Public Policy*, by Robert Pirog.

[28] Another argument is that the federal gas tax should be viewed as correcting the externalities associated with gasoline- powered vehicles. Even if the gas tax were to be viewed as one correcting for emissions, it would make more economic sense to tax emissions rather than just those coming from the burning of fossil fuels by motor vehicles.

[29] Tax expenditures are government revenue losses attributable to tax provisions that allow for special exclusions, exemptions, or deductions from income or provisions that provide special tax credits, preferential tax rates, of defer tax liability. Technically, excise tax credits are not considered tax expenditures because they do not directly impact income tax liability.

[30] The tax expenditure for percentage depletion is computed by subtracting the value of cost depletion, the standard depletion method, from the value of percentage depletion. The resulting lifetime excess is the tax expenditure.

[31] Expensing costs means to deduct the full cost of an investment in the current tax year, rather than depreciate the costs over a period of time.

[32] *De minimis* tax expenditures are not listed in **Table 1**.

[33] For more information, see CRS Report R40662, *Clean Coal Authorizations, Appropriations, and Incentives*, by Anthony Andrews and Molly F. Sherlock.

[34] See CRS Report R41635, *ARRA Section 1603 Grants in Lieu of Tax Credits for Renewable Energy: Overview, Analysis, and Policy Options*, by Phillip Brown and Molly F. Sherlock.

[35] Projects eligible for the PTC can claim the credit for 10 years. Thus, as projects that began construction before the end of 2011 but are placed in service in 2013 elect to receive a grant rather than claim the PTC, PTC claims in the out years will be less than what they would have been in absence of the grant program.

[36] See CRS Report R41573, *Tax-Favored Financing for Renewable Energy Resources and Energy Efficiency*, by Molly F. Sherlock and Steven Maguire.

[37] QECBs can be used to finance a broad range of energy efficiency and renewable energy projects. Eligible projects include energy efficiency upgrades for public buildings, renewable energy projects (including those eligible for CREBs), energy research and development projects, mass commuting facilities, and energy efficiency education campaigns.

[38] Official data on QECB issuances is not publicly available. The Energy Programs Consortium tracks known issuances of QECBs. See Energy Programs Consortium, *Qualified Energy Conservation Bonds (QECBs)*, Washington, DC, June 28, 2013, http://www.energyprograms.org/2013/06/qecb-paper/.

[39] More information on non-tax incentives can be found in CRS Report R42566, *Alternative Fuel and Advanced Vehicle Technology Incentives: A Summary of Federal Programs*, by Lynn J. Cunningham et al. and CRS Report R40168, *Alternative Fuels and Advanced Technology Vehicles: Issues in Congress*, by Brent D. Yacobucci.

[40] More information on qualifying vehicles and phase outs can be found at http://www.irs.gov/Businesses/Plug-In- Electric-Vehicle-Credit-%28IRC-30-and-IRC-30D%29.

[41] The majority of energy-related publicly traded partnerships are for activities in fossil fuels sectors. For more information, see CRS Report R41893, *Master Limited Partnerships: A Policy Option for the Renewable Energy Industry*, by Molly F. Sherlock and Mark P. Keightley.

[42] The cost of these incentives is as scored by the Joint Committee on Taxation (JCT).

[43] Similar proposals have been included in past Obama Administration budget proposals. For additional background, see CRS Report R42374, *Oil and Natural Gas Industry Tax Issues in the FY2013 Budget Proposal*, by Robert Pirog.

[44] For additional background on the Section 199 production activities deduction, see CRS Report R41988, *The Section 199 Production Activities Deduction: Background and Analysis*, by Molly F. Sherlock. Since this provision is widely available, and not specific to the energy industry, it is not listed in **Table 1**.

[45] The purpose of this proposal is to ensure that oil from tar sands are subject to the OSLTF excise tax. See CRS Report R43128, *Oil Sands and the Oil Spill Liability Trust Fund: The Definition of "Oil" and Related Issues for Congress*, by Jonathan L. Ramseur.

[46] Unlike the Superfund excise taxes, the corporate environmental income tax has no direct connection to past or current pollution or polluting activities.

[47] U.S. Congress, Joint Committee on Taxation, *Estimated Budget Effects of the Revenue Provisions Contained in the President's Fiscal Year 2014 Budget Proposal*, committee print, 113th Cong., May 10, 2013, JCX-11-13.

[48] More information on expiring tax incentives can be found in CRS Report R43124, *Tax Provisions Expiring in 2013 ("Tax Extenders")*, by Molly F. Sherlock.

[49] For background information on tax reform broadly, see CRS Report R43060, *Tax Reform in the 113th Congress: An Overview of Proposals*, by Molly F. Sherlock.

[50] A summary of these comments can be found in U.S. Congress, Joint Committee on Taxation, *Report to the House Committee on Ways and Means on Present Law and Suggestions for Reform Submitted to the Tax Reform Working Groups*, committee print, 113th Cong., May 6, 2013, JCS-3-13.

[51] Senate Committee on Finance tax reform options papers can be found at http://www.finance.senate.gov/issue/?id= 6c61b1e9-7203-4af0-b356-357388612063.

[52] A comprehensive list of all pending energy tax legislation in the 113th Congress is beyond the scope of this report. The proposals included in this section represent prominent energy-tax initiatives. A number of other energy tax-related bills introduced to date in the 113th Congress propose to extend, expand, or create specific energy-related tax provisions.

[53] For background, see CRS Report R42731, *Carbon Tax: Deficit Reduction and Other Considerations*, by Jonathan L. Ramseur, Jane A. Leggett, and Molly F. Sherlock.

[54] The full text of this discussion draft and supporting documents can be found at http://democrats.energycommerce.house.gov/index.php?q=news/waxman-whitehouse-blumenauer-and-schatz-release- carbon-price-discussion-draft.

[55] For background, see CRS Report R41893, *Master Limited Partnerships: A Policy Option for the Renewable Energy Industry*, by Molly F. Sherlock and Mark P. Keightley.

[56] For background and other legislation containing similar proposals see CRS Report R43128, *Oil Sands and the Oil Spill Liability Trust Fund: The Definition of "Oil" and Related Issues for Congress*, by Jonathan L. Ramseur.

[57] The alcohol fuel mixture tax credit, which became law in 2005, has been the source of controversy as the credit has been claimed by a number of paper companies that burn "black liquor," a practice that was not anticipated when the legislation was drafted. When the credit was initially enacted, it was expected to cost less than $100 million annually. During the first 6 months of 2009, more than $2.5 billion has been claimed for this tax credit. For more information see Martin A. Sullivan, "IRS Allows New $25 Billion Tax Break for Paper Industry," *Tax Notes*, October 19, 2009, pp. 271-272 and Chuck O'Toole, "Baucus, Grassley Draft Bill to End 'Black Liquor' Subsidy," *Tax Notes*, June 15, 2009, pp. 1312-1313.

[58] There is an important economic distinction between a subsidy and a tax benefit. As is discussed elsewhere in this report, firms receive a variety of tax benefits that are not necessarily targeted subsidies (or tax expenditures) because they are available generally.

[59] See CRS Report RL34696, *The 2008 Farm Bill: Major Provisions and Legislative Action*, coordinated by Renée Johnson for a complete description of the provisions in the 2008 Farm Bill.

[60] For cellulosic ethanol, the value of the cellulosic biofuel production credit is reduced by the value of the ethanol blender's credit and the small ethanol producer credit—so that the combined value of the credits equals $1.01. Thus, the credit for cellulosic ethanol is currently $0.46 per gallon ($1.01 minus $0.45 minus $0.10 [the small ethanol producer credit]). If the blender's credit and small ethanol producer credit were reduced (or

eliminated), the value of the cellulosic ethanol production credit would increase to keep the combined value at $1.01.

[61] For information on all energy provisions in ARRA see CRS Report R40412, *Energy Provisions in the American Recovery and Reinvestment Act of 2009 (P.L. 111-5)*, coordinated by Fred Sissine.

[62] The renewable energy PTC for wind facilities was extended through 2012.

[63] Prior to ARRA, the credit rate was 10%.

[64] Prior to ARRA, the credit caps ranged from $50 to $300, depending on the type of property installed. The credit was limited to $500 total for the 2006 and 2007 tax years combined. The credit was not available in 2008. The $1,500 limit applies to cumulative spending in the 2009 and 2010 tax years.

[65] See Martin A. Sullivan, "IRS Allows New $25 Billion Tax Break for Paper Industry," Tax Notes, October 19, 2009, pp. 271-272 for additional information concerning the original legislative intent of the modification of the alternative fuels tax credit in SAFETEA-LU. When enacted, the modification to the alternative fuels tax credit was estimated to cost less than $100 million annually. During the first six months of 2009, more than $2.5 billion were claimed for this tax credit, mostly by the paper industry. In addition, the Joint Committee on Taxation estimated that $23.6 billion will be saved between 2010-2019 from excluding black liquor from the cellulosic biofuel producers credit.

[66] U.S. Congress, Senate Committee on Finance, "Baucus, Grassley Release Staff Draft of Legislation to Close Alternative Fuels Tax Credit Loophole," press release, June 11, 2009, http://finance.senate.gov/press/Gpress/2009/ prg061109.pdf.

[67] Ibid.

[68] See Joint Committee on Taxation, JCX-17-10, available at http://www.jct.gov/ publications. html?func=showdown& id=3672.

[69] These credits were extended at a reduced rate, 10% as opposed to 30%. The limit associated with the credit was also reduced, from $1,500 to $500. Property specific caps for certain types of investments were reinstated.

[70] For more information, see CRS Report R42894, *An Overview of the Tax Provisions in the American Taxpayer Relief Act of 2012*, by Margot L. Crandall-Hollick.

INDEX

J

K

L

M

N

O

P

R

S

W